ABOUT THE AUTHOR

Seamus Lynch serves on the Vocations Ministry Group of the Presentation Brothers, and was an early participant on the Order's pioneering "Give a Year to God" scheme in the 1990s. A Masters in Economics during that time led to a teaching role at UCC and a subsequent career in advertising and media, culminating in his current position as Head of Media Research at TV3. His varied experience of youth issues ranges from surveys of 18-24s with MRBI and Amarach Consulting to crisis pregnancy counselling with Cura.

CAST OUT INTO THE DEEP

Attracting Young People to the Church

Seamus Lynch

The Liffey Press

Published by
The Liffey Press
Ashbrook House
10 Main Street
Raheny, Dublin 5, Ireland
www.theliffeypress.com

A catalogue record of this book is
available from the British Library.

ISBN 1-904148-58-1

Printed in Spain by GraphyCems.

CONTENTS

ACKNOWLEDGEMENTS

To my wife Ethna (and baby Rebecca): your patience and support, as always, was limitless.

To Aisling Cuddigan, Gerard Cloonan, Derek McGarrigle and their terrific pupils in Youghal, Athenry and Swords respectively: you gave this book the "X" factor that made its publication possible.

To Brother Martin Kenneally and the Presentation Brothers: it feels good to start giving you something back.

To people like Seamus Allard, Fr Martin O'Connor, Fr Brian D'Arcy and Kevin Doran who went the extra mile.

To Simon Rowe for kindly writing the Foreword.

To David and Brian at The Liffey Press for being as efficient as you were and a pleasure to work with.

To Ciara Considine, Jane, Shannon, Louisa, Fr Johnie, Tommy and Bríd, Dearbhail, Dylan, Mark Judy and Clement — and all those who encouraged and prayed for this book at various stages.

To each and every contributor — thank you.

FOREWORD

*Simon Rowe**

*C*ast Out into the Deep is an appropriate title for this book. In it, Seamus Lynch casts his net wide and deep, endeavouring to find answers that will help guide the Catholic Church in its quest to attract a new generation of young people in the twenty-first century.

This innovative volume takes a fresh approach to the challenge of evangelisation in Ireland. Its starting point is practical, not theoretical. It is driven not by an answer but by a question: "If you had to suggest one idea which might attract young people to the Church, what might it be?"

Directing this question to over 100 famous and not-so-famous people in Ireland, *Cast Out into the Deep* is a compendium of their responses. As such, it is an impressive "catch" of ideas and suggestions that should usefully

---

* Simon Rowe is a former Editor of *The Irish Catholic*. He has a background in business journalism, having worked as a journalist with *Business & Finance* magazine and as a radio producer with NewsTalk 106FM in Dublin. He holds a BA in History and Politics from University College Dublin.

form the basis of a strategy for evangelisation in the years ahead.

Cast Out into the Deep is an opportune book, coming at a time when a great number of young people seem to be disconnected from the Church. It implicitly asks: Why is there such a "disconnection" between the Church and young people and how can Church leaders help to bridge the gap?

It does not set about proposing a solution, confirming a particular thesis, or advocating any singular approach to evangelisation, however. It simply allows the ideas to speak for themselves. In later chapters, young people are asked to judge the various ideas on their merits and to make suggestions themselves. The end result is a book that provides a unique insight into the challenges facing the Church as it tries to dialogue with young people.

But as with any dialogue, for it to be constructive, it must be a two-way process. Therefore the Church must be both a teaching Church (*Ecclesia docens*) and a listening Church (*Ecclesia dicens*).

Writing in *Crossing the Threshold of Hope*, Pope John Paul II says that before beginning a dialogue with young people, the Church must have "a profound understanding of what it means to be young, of the importance that youth has for every person". By this, the Holy Father means the Church must recognise and foster young people's search for the meaning of life and propose to them a concrete way to go about living their life. Likewise too, the Pope says it is "necessary that the young know the Church, that they perceive Christ in the Church".

From the evidence of this volume, young people are very keen to play their part in this new dialogue with the Church, and to go in search of the meaning of life — together. These pages resound with the sound of dialogue.

Cast Out into the Deep is a timely book for another reason too. Arguably, never before have young people been in such need of what the Church has to offer. At a time when science and secularism seem to want to banish God to the margins of human life, young people's desire for universal values needs strong encouragement. At a time when virtually every moral position is assumed to be negotiable, the Church's message of eternal truths remains attractive and necessary. And at a time of media saturation, when young people are drowning in information but thirsting for meaning, they need to know that their lives have meaning and that that meaning is found in the Church.

Nobody can deny that many young Catholics today are "disconnected" from the Church. Whether this is mainly due to ignorance or indifference is a moot point. It's rare to find a young person who is "anti-Church", however. Perhaps what is lacking is that they have never before had the faith proposed to them in an attractive way. If this is the case, then now is the time for Church leaders to propose the faith once more to young people. To paraphrase Pope John Paul, the current generation of young people in Ireland is like a "continent waiting to be discovered", ready to be won for Christ.

But if the Church wants to "discover" this continent of young people, it must first rediscover its "pioneering spirit" of evangelisation. Somewhat like the old Wild West in America, the Irish Church needs to move from being a community of settlers to being a community of pioneers once again. A "New World" is out there waiting to be colonised for Christ. And as the title of this book suggests, it is well and truly time for Catholics to "launch out into the deep and let down the nets for a catch".

INTRODUCTION

ONE OF THE PURPOSES of the Vocations Ministry Group, on which I serve, is to brainstorm. Brainstorming is not just another corporate term for corporate ends: it can be applied quite comfortably and effectively to evangelisation and recruitment in a religious context. This book is essentially a brainstorming session with the aim of generating ideas for two main purposes:

- Increasing interest in the Church among young people and

- Achieving greater success for those involved in passing on Church-based values to young people.

Why is such a book necessary? It is partly because, 25 years after the current Pope's first visit to these shores, those within and without the Catholic Church have bandied about the word "crisis"; partly because the proposed second Papal visit provides the Church with an excellent opportunity to take stock of "where it's at" and build some momentum; and partly because enough people care, and are concerned enough, to help put a volume like this together.

In 2004, arguably the best publicity the Church received was for Mel Gibson's film *The Passion of the Christ*. It proved that it is still possible to absorb young people for two hours with religious material. Yet it fell into our laps and the cinemas of the nation in 2004 like manna from heaven. The challenge this book presents is to reproduce and build on the fervour in youth generated by a Papal visit or *The Passion of the Christ* on a more consistent basis.

I asked many people how to achieve this. As Desmond Cardinal Connell's contribution urges, I "put out into the deep". The nets I cast were humble. But the catch, from established vessels like the *Irish Catholic*, *Alive*, the *Irish Examiner* and the *Evening Herald*, as well as specifically targeted "fishers of men" was most heartening.

The constant question I posed was as follows:

> "If you had to suggest *one idea* which might strengthen young people's commitment to the Church, what would it be?"

The majority of answers are presented in Part 1, and the ensuing collection of ideas gathered is summarised in Part 2, by what is called "A New 95 Theses". To close the journey aptly, I felt it was necessary to involve young people directly. A questionnaire based on the 95 assembled "theses" helped to ascertain their views. The assistance of the teachers and 446 pupils in Swords, Athenry and

Youghal, in this regard, was priceless. It was somewhat amusing to see students essentially marking the work of older generations; their assessment of the ideas resulted in an ocean of statistics, the essence of which is presented in Part 3 with some concluding remarks.

Infamous, famous or not so famous, I extend my sincere gratitude to each and every one of my contributors. I am honoured by their representation here. To quote St Peter in Luke 5:9, I was "exceedingly amazed at the catch" from what was an enjoyable, year-long fishing expedition. Hopefully, you will conclude that this end product you hold in your hands justifies the trip!

For queries regarding this book and its contents, please contact the author at project2004ad@hotmail.com

Part 1

CASTING OUT:
A VARIETY OF VIEWS

When [Jesus] had finished speaking he said to Simon, "Put out into deep water and lower your nets for a catch." Simon replied, "Master, we worked hard all night and caught nothing. But if you say so, I will lower the nets." This they did and caught such a large number of fish that their nets began to break. They signalled their partners in the other boat to come and help them. They came and helped fill both boats almost to the point of sinking.

Upon seeing this, Simon Peter fell at Jesus' knees, saying, "Leave me Lord, for I am a sinful man!" For he and his companions were exceedingly amazed at the catch they had made. — Luke 5:4–9

LIST OF CONTRIBUTORS

Fr Seamus Ahearne OSA PP
Rivermount Parish, Dublin

Young people and the Church or young people and God?
Young ones (and older ones) will avoid the Church and
God if we seem prosaic and wooden and we sometimes
do! There is a surfeit of bad theology about and some of
it emanates from Rome. "God" is often protected in case
"he" might dirty "himself" in the dust of life/feelings/
realities of ordinary people. Rome has a profound regard
for tidy and archaic language to wrap up God and keep
him safe, which is hardly necessary. The "holy" has to be
rooted and grounded in our world. If God is not "at
home" in our world, then something has gone very
wrong and Jesus Christ has got it very wrong. We don't
really need the young ones to come back to us but rather
need to rediscover "youthfulness" in ourselves. I always
believe that if we take the incarnation seriously, then
everything else changes.

　We must delve into the imagination to catch things of
the Spirit and many of us are uncomfortable in that
arena. The world of art and mystery and beauty whispers
hints of the "rumours of angels". What did Schillebeeckx
say of the sacraments? A smile on the face of God! If we
could taste a little of that, we would be on the real pilgrimage of the traveller (in faith). God is always attractive (whatever about the Church). We don't have to pro-

tect God from the dangerous questions that the wonderful youngsters might throw at us — God can handle anything. So why do we seem to lack imagination and theology? So often when we are afraid or unsure, we hide in
the long grass of the past. The whole male priestly caste
is marvellous at control and organisation but is not too
good at handling mystery. It needs to be dismantled. We
are caught up with false problems and historical anoma-
lies, which distract us from much more important issues
("fiddling while Rome burns" comes to mind).

I am always aware that the big questions of life take
energy and toughness of spirit. It takes maturity to enter
this world. Young people now are more prone to easy
solutions and easy boredom. They want the immediate
(and often superficial!). They are at home with the Sky
News question of the day, which only requires a yes/no
answer! Real life asks much more from us. So I do have a
real question for young people. Can you really handle the
important issues or have you got only a wishbone for a
backbone.

The Church does need to be more direct and less
apologetic. The Church has carried this country for generations and has given (and gives) too much. If we truly
are believers — then we will be confident! We can ask the
bigger questions. There is a real lack of serious reflection
in our society and we must be robust and ruthless in
provoking serious questions. The media isn't doing it
and possibly can't. The media has to be popular, as do
the politicians. Faith people can't succumb to the same
temptation, which runs from real issues! We need to ac-

cept the privileged and dangerous task (like the writer Graham Greene) to observe and challenge. God deserves such rigour from us. Too much Church commentary is weak and self-interested.

We failed in our response to the sex abuse problem but we can learn from it. We have allowed ourselves to become the victim (cheap scapegoat for sloppy journalists) and thereby to be institutionally abused. This holds us up to ridicule, which hardly makes us "cool" and attractive for young people to get involved with us. We have work to do and changes to make. We cannot become a museum for visiting or observing but rather an energetic, imaginative and youthful community full of artistic excitement where the young are really at home and find space for their enthusiasm and ideals. If we remain as we are — they shouldn't bother. I would be concerned for any young person who might at present be becoming involved in Church life unless some big changes happen. And yet I know that there is no better place to be or more exciting possibilities anywhere when the Spirit is let loose and the incarnation is actually celebrated. Jesus Christ deserves imagination from us all to move forward and into the real counter-cultural mode that is essential. There is a job to do and we must do it now.

Nora Bennis
Leader of the National Party

I am of the opinion that young people today will be attracted to the Church and committed to her service, only in as much as they can see that the Church is prepared to stand up for and defend their fundamental right to have their *basic needs* provided for. You see, no matter what social changes take place around us, children's fundamental or basic needs remain the same as ever. The singularly most important of these is the need for the young child to have a central figure in their life whose responses show that they are special and from whom they will only grow away *gradually*. This is true for all children, in all places and at all times. This central figure, with few exceptions, is the child's mother. There is no substitute for a mother who is bonded to and loves her child, and sociologists and enlightened people generally agree that for a mother to function best she needs a good man at her side who loves her and respects her unconditionally. We are talking here about a child's basic need for their family. Question: When young people look at the Church today, do they see a Church that unequivocally proclaims and affirms this basic need? Do they see a Church that is not afraid to challenge a system that is hostile to this basic need? Do they see a Shepherd or a hireling?

If the Church authorities in Ireland take seriously the statement by the Holy Father that "the future of the

world passes by way of the family", and if the Church authorities *demonstrate by their actions* that they truly
believe this fundamental truth, if Mother Church com-
mits herself to the protection and defence of the family
based on marriage, I believe young people will be more
than generous in their response. The Catechism of the
Catholic Church describes the family as the *domestic*
church. It declares that, "A man and a woman united in
marriage, together with their children, form a family."

I was one among hundreds of people who in 1994
were invited to Dublin Castle to celebrate the launch of
the UN International Year of the Family. We heard the
Minister for Social Welfare proudly announce that the
Irish Government had embraced the UN technical definition of the family, which is:

> "Any combination of two or more persons who
> are bound together by ties of mutual consent,
> birth and/or adoption or placement and who
> together assume responsibility for, inter alia,
> the care and maintenance of group members,
> the addition of group members through pro-
> creation or adoption, the socialisation of
> children and the social control of its members."

The UN understanding of family could never adequately
provide for the basic needs of the child. Young people today know, and I believe, that given half a chance, young
people will follow the leader who is not afraid to stand up
and defend their fundamental rights to have their basic
needs supplied. Young people will commit themselves to
a Church that has committed itself to them.

Sr Eilis Bergin

*Presentation Sister; Director of Retreats;
Teacher, and Co-author of* The Enneagram

I was fortunate to enjoy a wonderful youth in Ireland during the sixties. These days I am moved and challenged by the energy and dynamism of young people. They are growing up in a chaotic world where it can be hard to find any point of reference or any security. My wish for them is that they would meet dynamic and committed people who would inspire them to get in touch with the beauty, giftedness and potential that is theirs. I would urge them to seek out ways to express their Christian beliefs through involvement with groups who make the mission of Jesus real in today's world.

During my first month at the retreat house here, I met two teenage schoolboys who had returned from a visit to Calcutta in India where they had spent some time helping the poor. This experience had brought their faith to life and had a great influence on their classmates.

My message to young people today: "You are precious. Believe in yourself and share your gifts with others."

Fr Harry Bohan
Shannon Parish, County Clare

One idea: my idea of what Church is about begins with "where people are at" and how it can help to connect people, including young people with Christian values. For this to happen, people in this Church need to be real, authentic, honest and involved in a deep relationship with Christ, while walking the journey with people — listening to their stories.

Finally, I would invite young people to help us, adults, as in helping parents to parent, etc.

Fr Con Breen CC
Howth Parish

Take the Sacrament of Confirmation out of the primary schools — and, indeed, out of the school altogether. Let the Sacrament be given around 16 years of age, and organised through the parishes. In order to qualify for the Sacrament, the young people would have to do a course of preparation in the local parish over a period to be set down. Perhaps a common national date could be designated (e.g. Pentecost Sunday) as the suitable date for Confirmation Sunday. Details might differ in different circumstances, but of the general idea, I am very deeply convinced.

If only the bishops were prepared to "cast out into the deep"! I am also convinced that there are a considerable number of young people like yourself, who are convinced likewise, that the onus of passing on the Faith in our country depends on them. If only those who today are in positions of power would give them — the young people — the opportunity to respond.

Michael Breen

Head of Department, Media and Communications, Mary Immaculate College, University of Limerick

We can often despair about our empty churches and our declining congregations and can readily blame our young people, or our changing culture or the media or material prosperity — anything in fact but ourselves. We need to take a long hard look at ourselves, and our reality as the Church — do we in fact proclaim in our lives, again and again and again, the great message of salvation in Christ, not as something to come but as something lived here and now? Is there anything attractive and compelling about the Christ to whom we witness on a day-to-day basis in our lives?

Imagine what the Church might be like:

- If every member of it took the message of salvation seriously

- If we were a community focused on the Gospel of Christ Jesus, and committed to putting it into action

- If it was a place where worship of the living God was vibrant and alive — a collection of people whose love and compassion were evident for all to see

- Where people were given priority over possessions

- Where primary needs took precedence over indulgent wants

- Where life was lived to the full in God's image and likeness

- Where challenge and possibility and growth and freedom were at the core

- Where the very presence of the Lord Jesus was tangible.

The real invitation of the scriptures is to dream a dream: to reflect on what a vibrant Church focused on the Risen Christ would look and feel like, and how the world in which such a Church was active might be different from the status quo. How would our worship be different? What would it mean to be a member of such a community? What would it take? What might it cost us? What would its promise be for the world? How would the status quo change?

But perhaps the crucial question is a little different: do we really want a Church like that? Really? There is something very unthreatening about things as they are. Looking at a new vision raises enormous questions about challenge and commitment and involvement. It is light years away from a Church of complacency where we can come along for a few moments on a Sunday and delude ourselves that we have lived the Gospel for another week. Such a powerful vision of the Church is certainly discomfiting. It demands accountability; it provides challenge as well as care; it calls us to put our money where our mouths are: to put our time, talent and treasure at the disposal of others for the sake of the common good.

Change at a communal level will not come unless individual hearts are moved to change. It is always easy to wring our hands in despair, to talk about what things might be like if only somebody else would do something, to sit back and pick holes in every effort that is made by others. But the urgency of the Gospel calls us to leave such commentary behind, to get stuck in and get our own hands dirty, to accept the urgency of our task and to go about the business of proclaiming and living this Gospel of the Risen Christ.

The Gospel issues you with a direct challenge as a believer: in what way will you share your time, your treasure and your talent, for the welfare of the Church and the world? You are being called to be of service, you are being called to get involved, you are being called to be a bearer of the good news of the Gospel, of hope, of reconciliation, of possibility. Whose life will be touched by your response to the call of Jesus Christ? What difference will you make?

As I now sit in the pews on Sundays, I find to my absolute horror that most preaching I hear is (a) mostly abysmal (b) often heretical (c) commonly ignorant of the Gospel and (d) rarely Christocentric. But the larger vision of being Church is so absent. Part of the difficulty is that there is no place else to go, but I've come to the conclusion that it's my Church too, and that I will not let the "others" take over.

Debbie Brennan
Independent Newspapers

Priests should be allowed to marry, then they will have the experience and proper knowledge when giving advice about marriage, relationships, etc. I do not attend Church. I find it quite boring and a waste of time. However, I do believe in God and do pray to my Angels. I do not take into consideration what priests preach!

I am 25 years old and have just got married. If we do have children, I will take them to Church to pray, but not to Mass. I will teach them what I know about the Bible, which was taught to me by my parents/grandmother/ school. I will tell them the importance of the Ten Commandments, Holy Communion and Confirmation. I would definitely attend Mass if the following changes were made:

- Priests to marry
- The format of the Mass to change:
  - Introduction and prayers
  - Speak about what's happening in the community/ news
  - People to stand up and give their views

o   Person of the parish (not a priest/nun) to speak
    after the Gospel about a personal experience, etc.
    (different person each week)

o   Holy Communion and close: lots of singing, clap-
    ping and basically just a good and interesting at-
    mosphere!

Other proposed ideas: Gospel choirs, summer projects
and evening social clubs.

Most Rev John Buckley DD
Bishop of Cork and Ross

There is a good degree of commitment by young people to the Church at present. That point needs to be made from the outset because there seems to be an impression that young people are not interested in Church. That is not my experience.

From travelling to the parishes in this diocese at weekends, I always encounter many young people at Mass in every parish. That, of course, is not the full picture. Second- and third-level chaplains encounter and support young people on a regular basis and many young people, through school or local groups, are involved in the Lord's work in their own locality.

However, one of the biggest challenges facing the Church in Ireland is how that commitment can be strengthened. There are a variety of answers and a multiplicity of approaches. First of all, that commitment must be nurtured, nourished, supported and strengthened at local level. I am referring here to the local parish. Parishes that have invited young people to become involved at a liturgical and parish council level have been enriched by the contributions made and it must be said that the young people and their faith commitment have benefited too. That is a critical point. Faith is always supported when it is given a means of expression. That is true of every generation.

The second point is equally important. The contribution of young people must be respected, and valued. In other words, the involvement must not be lip service! In this diocese at present we are involved in a consultative process concerning the way forward involving three representatives from each parish; one of these representatives is always a young person. The contribution of young people must always be encouraged and sought. That is a challenge for all involved in Church. The task may be difficult at times but it is essential and vital for the life of the Church in the years to come.

The Vatican Documents, particularly *Ad Gentes Divinitas* — the decree on the Church's missionary activity — stresses that the whole Church is missionary in nature. Pope John Paul said that young people represented another continent to be evangelised for Christ. That is the challenge for priests and bishops. We must get young people involved at every level and when they are involved, we must keep encouraging that involvement, listen to what is being said and try to take these views on board. The task is a big one but an important one. After all, ecclesiastical unemployment leads to spiritual emigration!

Fr Martin Byrne CFC
Author of Unmasking God
(on inner city youth)

I am writing from the stance of someone born, raised and now working with youth in Dublin's north inner city. Young people's commitment would be strengthened if they experienced the radical values of Jesus' Gospel in their engagements with the people, rituals, language and culture of the Church.

If the Church captured God's Dream, then . . .

In the world of inner city youth where society and church sometimes treat our kids as if they were nobodies, "scum" or deficient . . .

Jesus' Church would demonstrate that each youngster is special, that the stirrings of their spirit are sacred and that their voice is to be heard.

In the world of inner city youth, which is often cluttered with noise and with globalised packaged answers . . .

Jesus' Church would gift these youngsters with tools for reflection, oases of silence, respectful listening ears, unsettling awkward questions and with a treasury of searchers' wisdom.

In the world of inner city youth, so full of traumatic changes, seductive developments and the accepted myth of prosperity . . .

Jesus' Church would in simple solidarity with the poor challenge the world-view and the injustice of society's powerful.

In the world of inner city youth, which is familiar with failure, enmeshments and drug-induced death . . .

Jesus' Church would enliven our imaginations with the story of Jesus, freeing us to touch into our own pains and encouraging us to live deeper in our own humanity and to see beyond the "Five Lamps".

In the world of inner city youth, which is at times alienated, angry and passive . . .

Jesus' Church would affirm the many local heroes of compassion and be an architect locally of an atmosphere of gratefulness and dependence on a Loving God.

In the world of inner city youth where the "I" of individualism requires attention . . .

Jesus' Church would validate the strong communal ethic and the traditional neighbourly values in the local culture, which are under threat.

Vanessa Conneely
Freelance Journalist

In terms of recruiting new priests and nuns, I feel very strongly that the marriage ban should be lifted to encourage young people to join. I think the Church needs to reinvent the way it teaches young people. Forcing them to pray and attend Mass is no longer something which youngsters can relate to. I think encouraging religion to be discussed — rather than taught — in schools from a very young age is vital because young people nowadays live in a world where they are told to question everything.

Drugs, bullying, sex, etc., are all issues that cannot be dealt with by forcing a Bible down a young child's throat. However, discussing the spiritual side to religion and actively allowing children to take part in retreats and exercises would be a new approach and a step forward to allowing them to tell the Church what they need.

The Church needs to be more passive rather than aggressive in its approach to young people and needs to listen rather than to judge. Perhaps an approach which combines priests and nuns with community centres and counsellors might help the current situation.

Desmond Cardinal Connell
Retired Archbishop of Dublin

I think that the simplest way of responding to your request is to send you copies of an article I published in *The Irish Times* on 21 February 2001 and the homily that I preached on my return to Dublin after the Consistory. The early part of the homily refers to the Pope's Apostolic Letter *Novo Millennio Ineunte*. The article sums up very briefly the essence of my message as a bishop. Perhaps you will be able to find something in these texts to assist you.

With kind wishes
Yours sincerely
Desmond Cardinal Connell

Below is an edited version of the Cardinal's enclosed texts.

At the end of the Jubilee Year 2000, which marked the second Millennium of the coming of Christ, the Holy Father wants to help us go forward on the path marked out by the jubilee experience. In his letter *Novo Millennio Ineunte* he offers guidance for the journey before us.

There are challenges, difficulties and opportunities for the Church in Ireland. But we can deal with the problems and make the most of the opportunities only by finding our centre and setting out from there. For the Christian, the centre is the person of Christ.

At the heart of Christian faith there is a mystical call addressed to us all and not just to the saints. It has to do with "the knowledge of Christ". This is not knowledge about Christ such as scholars may acquire through research, whether or not they have faith. It resembles much more the personal knowledge that grows out of our human experience of friendship. As St Augustine says, "One comes to know a person only through friendship" (*De Div Quaest.LXXI:5*).

The uniqueness of Christ is clear from this: that he alone of all the figures of history is loved; loved through the centuries by succeeding generations in the church. He can be known in the love of friendship precisely because he is alive.

Knowledge of Christ is the life of the church, and it is shared by all that live the life of the church.

The Irish Times, 21 February 2001

Extracts from Homily at Reception in the Pro Cathedral following the Consistory, 4 March 2001:

"You have made us for yourself, O Lord, and our heart is restless until it rests in you" (St Augustine, *Confessions*, 1,1).

These are the words of St Augustine. He spent the years of his youth in the shallows until he heard God's voice calling him out into the deep: "Put out into the deep" (Luke 5:4). These words of Jesus to Peter are given us by Peter's Successor to guide us in the post-Jubilee years. Putting out into the deep means following Christ. But first we have to come to know him.

It makes us attentive to his word and witnesses to that word in the way we live. It means recognising his face in the face of our suffering and needy brothers and sisters, and serving them as he has served us.

Mary Coughlan TD
Minister for Social and Family Affairs

I had to ponder your question long and hard. In fact, it gave cause for some interesting discussion when I raised it with family and friends. It's a difficult question, and one to which there is perhaps no single answer, and I might have some other answers later in the year or later in life, but for now I would suggest a single word: participation.

By being involved, by participating, people will find themselves drawn into the Church — whether through more active participation in the Mass, through more discussion on the future role of the Church or through more contact with representatives of the Church. Those are just a few options for people, but we should not forget participation is for the Church too.

What has the Church done recently that made young people want to get involved, to identify with their Church? I would point to the many charitable acts of Bishop Willie Walsh, and many of his statements, as providing spiritual leadership and involvement, and participation in society.

Young people need role models and support in achieving similar status — participation is the key.

Fr Brian D'Arcy
St Gabriel's Retreat, County Fermanagh

Experience has taught me that we Church leaders are brilliant at giving comprehensive answers to questions no one is asking. So my suggestion would be to ask young people themselves. I'm too old to know what attracts young people today. Having asked them I would try to do what they suggested. To help you cast out into the deep, I actually got a group of young people together. This is part of what they reported back.

"In the Gospel tonight we, the young, have been told that we are the *light* of the world. Light is something we need just now. If we could brighten up the Church, the first thing we'd do would be to *ban* monotonous sermons and make it compulsory to add variety to the way we celebrate in Church."

"We'd insist on a variety of Church leaders, who would not necessarily be ordained; allow women to become priests. We'd allow priests the freedom to marry if they chose to and we'd have lots of young people giving Communion, reading and singing."

We'd put up big signs saying *For God's Sake Smile. Be Happy. Enjoy Your Faith.* Church is far too dull and serious. We should have a welcoming Church. A place we'd *love* to come to, *not* a place we *have* to come to."

"To make it a welcoming place we'd change some old-fashioned rules and we'd let people know they don't have to feel guilty. They don't have to be outcasts because they're not perfect. We'd stop interfering so much in people's personal lives."

"If Christ's message was really taken on board we'd have support groups for people in need:

- People with drug addiction

- Those caught up in violence

- People with AIDS

- Those in the Third World

- Those struggling with religion/faith."

"If everybody felt welcome, Churches would become more alive. Light gives out power. We as young people have a power of our own. We have the future in our hands. We *are* the future."

"We have drive, ambition, energy, youth. We have health, talent and ability. We can stand up for ourselves. We have the new ideas. We are a generation who is aware of what's going on around us and we can face the challenge to do something positive for the world we live in. As the saying goes, *Better to light one candle than to curse the darkness.*"

Regina Deacy

Member of the Irish Bishops Advisory Committee on Church Music and Music Director at Ballina Cathedral

Working with young people and the Church is certainly not an easy task, needing lots of patience and sometimes not seeing results of your work at all. The only hope is that they will remember some of what was passed on into adulthood and continue from there. It paid off with us (and our involvement with the Church) when we were students! I have a good few young people in the choir and through singing the word of God and attending Mass regularly, they are becoming committed. They are even raising issues and asking questions about things.

Monsignor Patrick Devine
Diocesan Secretary for Ecumenism, Dublin

Most young people are well disposed to religion and church life while attending primary school. The new challenges that come in early teens seem to require an appropriate social support group with which the over-13s can identify, and in which this initial goodwill can be fostered and matured.

A model that is somewhat on the same lines of what I have in mind already exists in the Colleges Volunteer Corps, a body which from 1961 until the present has done quite a lot of good in this area.

Fr Kevin Doran
National Vocations Co-ordinator

Decisions! Decisions! What will I wear? What will I
study? Who will I choose as my friend? How will I earn
some money? Whose advice will I trust? What will I do
about the pregnancy? To what will I commit my life?

Making choices and decisions is part and parcel of
life. As far as I can see, young people enjoy having the
freedom to make their own decisions, but they often find
decision-making difficult. They hope for happiness, but
they don't know how or where they can be sure of finding it. They don't like cheap imitations, but they are frequently offered superficial answers to life's questions.
They recognise that a great deal can hang on making the
right decision. They don't want other people to make
their decisions for them, but neither do they feel terribly
comfortable standing out from the crowd.

At the heart of the Church's faith is the idea that,
when he called us into life, God had something unique in
mind for each one of us, something which would lead to
our happiness and our fulfilment. I would like young
people to know that the Church cares deeply about their
happiness and, if there were one practical thing I could
do, I would like to share with them something of the
Church's wisdom about decision-making, which we call
discernment. It is a way of making life-choices, which

enhances our freedom, because it allows us to discover, and to become, more fully what we were created to be.

I was asked to write something about one idea that might strengthen young people's commitment to the Church. I believe that commitment is built on trust, and trust is the fruit of relationship, which has matured over time. The "idea" I have is not particularly original, but I think it may need to be re-discovered. It is about tapping into the real needs and heart-wishes of young people, supporting them in their decision-making in a way which respects and enhances their freedom, rather than stifling it. It is the kind of work which is already being done by diocesan youth services and vocations centres, but I believe we need to find a way to make it part of the ministry of every parish community.

Eamon Dunphy
Author, Journalist and Broadcaster with Newstalk 106

Rather than castigate young people for sinning, the Church might more usefully confirm that it believes in the essential decency of all who set out in the world. Most people want to be virtuous. On the whole, most young people are. If the Church was regarded as the enemy of the world's corrupting influences that would resonate with those who are young and idealistic.

Terence Fitzgerald
Third World Development Worker

I really wish I had something insightful, adroit, critical or even mordant to contribute to what I think is a very interesting concept — but I don't think I have. I have a variety of opinions on the institution — ranging from very positive views of, say, missionaries I've met in Sierra Leone and Kenya devoting their lives to the poor, to negative ones of unctuous bishops telling people that condoms don't reduce the risk of HIV/AIDS infection, for the sake of an abstracted principle.

Certainly, an increased focus on its work with the poor — both domestically and internationally — that, surely, would appeal to even the most cynical of hearts — combined with a greater recognition that the principles that they (rightly) stand for have to be tempered by the reality of people's lives.

Joseph Foyle
Foil the Devil Crusade

I choose to believe that the Devil exists. But I do not fear, because I do things that Christians do to foil him. There are things we can and should do with urgency to shield others, and therefore ourselves, from the Devil.

Our discussions find that few now do things to foil the Devil. Most people do not even think about him. Their preachers do not remind them enough. We invite individuals and groups to discuss how to foil the Devil, and go on to do so with steady enthusiasm.

It is not aimed specifically at young people though it is highly relevant, I think, to their needs. We cannot hope to enhance the Catholic practice of young people without also doing so, with the same motivation, for their parents and older relatives and friends.

Gerard Gallagher
World Youth Day Officer

I would propose that young people need a new and deeper challenge. I have found that when young people are challenged in faith, with the message and challenge of the Gospel, many say, "I did not know that" or "I have never heard about it before". Pope John Paul II has personally challenged young people with the Gospel with the World Youth Days. I have seen young people reflect on their faith differently after hearing him personally challenge them to live a life modelled on Jesus.

Throughout my work with young people over the last ten years, I have found that if young people are invited to reflect and learn about their faith, in small intimate groups, this challenge can be communicated. I have met some very courageous young people who have changed their lives after a deep and meaningful encounter with the Gospel. My one simple idea is for more people, priests and lay people, not to be afraid of communicating their faith to young people. Not everyone is able to work with young people. However, everyone can share their faith story.

Mary Hanafin TD
Minister of State, Department of the Taoiseach and Department of Defence

After 50 years of rapid social and cultural change in Irish society, we have to reappraise the values and norms that we once took for granted. One of the many questions facing us now is: where does the Church fit into this new culture? What role does it have to play now, especially in the lives of our younger people?

Today's 15-year-old is a different creature to that of 50, or even 20, years ago. They are growing up quicker, they are more independent, less likely to pay attention to role models of any sort, and more likely to succumb to peer pressure. With increasing levels of marital breakdown, family units are no longer as strong a support system as they once were. There is evidence that this increased independence and lessening of parental control is leading some young people to engage in risk behaviour, such as binge drinking and under-age sex. One of the more alarming indicators of young people's difficulty in accepting and adapting to social change is the phenomenal increase in the incidences of suicide among young men in the past fifteen years. There has been a 79 per cent increase in the number of young men committing suicide in Ireland since 1989.

There is clearly a vacuum in Irish society, and the challenge facing us now is what we choose to fill that vacuum. The Church and the Christian message it brings have something valuable to offer a changing Irish society and its younger people. The Church can act as a source of comfort in times of difficulty and offer hope for the future. The Christian message is that God will not bring you to what he cannot bring you through. Encouraging young people to live by Christian values is not a question of shunning modern values like consumerism but of re-discovering just how the two can live side by side. They don't have to be, nor can we afford for them to be, mutually exclusive. It is now time to focus on the basics, that which is at the heart of the Christian ethos — respect for self and for others, and a sense of social responsibility. Discovering just how to achieve this is the real challenge facing Irish society and the Church in the new century.

Fr Hugh Hanley SCJ
Sacred Heart Fathers/Dehonians and Project 2030

My idea — and this is what I do with the Project 2030 groups — is to get young people together and ask them what I can do to help them. One of their great needs is to socialise together, to be with others who are not embarrassed about being practising Catholics today. Most of the time they want to go for meals, walks, the cinema, etc. But they are also interested in retreats and pilgrimages. I try to facilitate their being together as best I can.

Sr Agnes Haverty
OLA Missionary, Argentina

My own one idea is that the Church which appeals to young people is the Church that moves out to meet the people instead of waiting for the people to come; the Church that is present among the poor and suffering — the sick, old, downtrodden, hungry, etc. — not as a judge but as a compassionate companion!

The answers of the youth here to your question basically come down to giving them space and responsibility — and one even said to take away the old people who want to control everything! They didn't say, "take them away" but "throw them out!"

Fr Sean Healy SMA
CORI Justice Commission

"Get a Life!"

In jest, have you ever told a friend to "get a life"? What does "having a life" mean to you? What would enhance the quality of your life? What would "having a life" mean to someone who is being bullied? What would it mean to someone who is poor? Or to someone who has a disability that hampers their participation? What would "having a life" mean to someone who is marginalised in society? Or to someone who is old and lonely?

In the Gospels, we read that Jesus told his followers that He had come to bring fullness of life to all of us (John 10:10). He did this through his work and teaching and finally though His death and resurrection. A follower of Jesus is called to bring life, to help others to "get a life". Part of the role of the Church that Jesus founded is to serve people so that all members can enjoy fullness of life and reach out in life-giving service to other people.

This is the "good news" that Jesus talked about (Luke 4:18). At the end of the day, can you go to sleep knowing that somebody has a little bit more of a life because of how you lived this day?

I believe that a Church that is focused on ensuring that all people (its own members and all other people as well) can have life and have it to the full is the kind of Church that will attract young people.

Florence Horsman Hogan
Co-founder, LOVE (Let Our Voices Emerge)

By now, those in religious life seem to have become fair game for any allegation. Unsubstantiated stories have become financially beneficial after documentaries and books have been presented to an unsuspecting public as fact.

I feel that if young people were made more aware of the scale of unsubstantiated abuse allegations, at least some of their cynicism concerning the Church and clerical abuse might be overcome.

Fr Michael Hurley
Cell Group Co-ordinator

Logic of the Heart

In 1983 the Western Irish Bishops wrote about the influences of cult groups, about what can be learned from their existence and what may be a response to them. These groups, they claimed, hint at a spiritual hunger among young people that is often unrecognised, and offer them a sense of belonging that they do not experience on Sunday. They conclude that "the best of what they experience outside the Church must be provided more widely within. If the temper of the times is for the companionship of small groups, the challenge to us is to expand and encourage such groups within the community of the Church."

Godfried Cardinal Danneels in *Christ or Aquarius* claimed that sects appeal largely because society is becoming "increasingly depersonalised. People are becoming mere numbers; rarely are they treated as people . . . this is where sects come on the scene. . . . They nourish the logic of the heart rather than that of the mind. And they let you know you are unique."

The above quotations, transcending the specific contexts, provide an insight into society today and the needs of the young for spirituality, companionship and belonging. Today the churches are not nourishing the logic of the heart nor of the mind. Many Irish parishes attest that they have seen a virtual disappearance of young adults from Sunday worship. Young people, apart from a very small percentage, are simply not finding in the churches what satisfies their yearnings. They tend to see that what is hosted by the church is irrelevant, outdated and authoritarian.

Cell Groups

In 13 years of association with cell groups in Ireland, I have seen their impact upon individuals of all age groups. Growing in friendship, searching together for meaning and deepening of commitment, are central experiences for those who participate. Cell groups are small faith groups of between four and twelve people who meet each fortnight in the homes of a participant. The format of a meeting comprise of a few hymns and an opening prayer, reflection on a scriptural passage, sharing about where one may have seen God's influence since the previous meeting, a brief talk explaining an aspect of faith, discussion upon what is heard, prayer of intercession and of healing.

These elements encourage people to reflect upon what faith means to them in the daily encounters and events of life and help them see its implications within home, neighbourhood, work, recreation and parish. Usually a number of things tend to happen. Firstly, people become good friends, alert to each other's wishes and needs. Young people, in particular, often speak of the importance, for them, of friendship within cell groups.

Secondly, there awakens a deeper and more personal sense of God present with them. Thirdly, people are encouraged to look beyond themselves in service of others. Cell groups differ from most faith groups in that they are committed to a culture of evangelisation, helping and forming individuals to share faith with others.

Recommendation

The experience of cell groups points towards the challenge of providing opportunities for young people to form friendships, reflect upon the meaning and purpose of life and engage in service and mission towards the world and its people. It thus posits the possible contribution of a forum for young people and young adults in local settings where they can relate in an atmosphere which is welcoming, reflective and facilitates commitment and service. It recognises in this the provision of a creative alternative within the dominant culture.

A difficulty may lie in initially catching the imagination of the young. Once imagination is engaged, youth are capable of enormous commitment. Michael Paul Gallagher believes that local faith settings are indeed necessary to fire and support imagination. "There is a battle," he claims, "for people's minds and hearts and imaginations. Individuals need the support of communities to forge a Christian option that can survive."

Barbara Johnston
Spokesperson for the National Congress of Catholic Secondary Schools Parents Association

You ask what would strengthen young people's commitment to the Church and I ask you what commitment? I cannot suggest ways to strengthen a commitment that in my opinion does not exist. I believe that young people see the teachings of the Church to be outdated and they see the actions of the Church to be less than truthful. They are more outspoken and better educated. They are not afraid to ask the questions we only thought about. They ask why priests cannot get married, why are women second-class citizens in the Church, what gives the Church the right to dictate on contraception and many other questions that have never really been answered.

The Church does not fit. It is not a comfortable garment they can go through life wearing — therefore many of them leave it behind.

Lorraine Keane
Columnist and TV Presenter

Priests should make more of an effort to make the Mass interesting by being more entertaining themselves. The altar is their stage. They are "presenters" of the word of God. They have a message to spread *and* they have a captive audience. Yet so many just read from the Bible and young people just switch off. If I was to present my news in the same way, do you think the audience would tune in the next day? I drive to Eadestown in Kildare (one hour by car) to attend Mass because the priest, Fr Sean Breen, gives Mass there. His Mass is an enjoyable experience, one I look forward to. I leave the church with a smile on my face and feel fulfilled at the same time.

Sr Stanislaus Kennedy
Author and Founder of Focus Ireland, The Sanctuary and Social Innovations Ireland

Young people need something tangible, credible, real and alive — they need a Church that speaks to them in a way that makes sense to their way of life. Young people like to be challenged — they need a Church that is visionary and challenges their commitment and generosity. Young people are idealistic — they need to express themselves through freedom and authenticity. Young people have huge energy and they need to express it in love of self and love of neighbour.

The Church needs to find ways of listening to the voice of young people, of forming partnerships with them, if it is to be relevant now and in the future.

Mary Kenny
Writer, Columnist with The Irish Catholic

I have felt for some time that music is very important, as it seems to be the international youth language these days. But I was dismayed to attend an Anglican church last Sunday with stunning music and there was *no one* else in the congregation.

I am beginning to think that really old-fashioned devotion, the more spiritual the better — pilgrimages, novenas and the cult of saints, including local saints — are absolutely vital.

I think devotions such as the Stations of the Cross are beautiful and enriching and provide the inner life of the faith.

Also, in Ireland, such traditions as blessing the home and even motor cars are very, very relevant. Hope this is of some assistance.

Fr Colm Kilcoyne PP
Cong Parish, and Spokesperson for the National Conference of Priests

A difficult question. I suspect that any worthwhile answer has to deal with involvement. Work they can get their teeth into.

One idea? That the Parish Council might have a strong active Youth Interest Group that would work with a person trained in the Gospel, trained in understanding youth and trained in planning, carrying out and assessing church-related projects for young people. Parishes (separately or in groups) would need to fund properly the work of these Youth Ministers. For this special ministry to be real, the overall parish background would need to be seen as a welcoming, non-judgemental place.

Rebecca Leavy
Irish Epilepsy Association, Galway

I think you should keep a number of things in mind. Firstly, please don't think of "young people" as being a homogenous group. Young people are individuals.

Secondly, you might want to think about what you mean by "attracting" young people. Does this mean getting young people to go to Mass? If so, I would rethink your strategy here. Lots of people would consider themselves to be spiritual/religious people, but choose not to go to Mass. This choice should be respected. Maybe the Catholic Church should think a bit more broadly about the various ways to practice religion, other than the traditional mass-going way.

It's important that you ask young people why they do or don't practise Catholicism. When did they stop practising and why? What would they change if they could change something within the Church or about the Mass? Do they pray? What do they think of the Catholic Church? Do they believe in God? What do they get from going to Mass? Does it bring them closer to God?

I think it would be good to get groups of young people together for a good, loud, heated debate. This could be done through schools, youth groups, after-schools clubs, etc. I would suggest that you try to get feedback from a broad range of backgrounds — middle class and working class, urban and rural, male and female, gay and straight, young teenagers and older teenagers, practising Catholics and non-practising Catholics. Make sure that everyone feels able to talk openly. There's bound to be some anti-Catholic opinions: you'll have to be prepared for this and accept it.

The most important thing is that young people are consulted. In order to decide how to attract young people, the Church must ask itself: why do they need to be attracted in the first place? In other words, what has the Church done or not done to cause so many young people to lose interest and/or faith in Catholicism?

Elizabeth Lev
Christian Art and Architecture Teacher, Rome

I wonder this often myself as I teach at a nominally Catholic school, but very few of my students have any idea of what it is that they are part of. I find that as we start the semester and talk about the martyrs, heroic resistance and unfaltering belief, they are fascinated. Much more moving to them than the lavish displays of gold-decked churches are the simple catacombs where millions of people have come to pay homage to a brave 13-year-old girl.

This is what I think is so special about *The Passion of the Christ* as well. Jesus is not portrayed as this "nice guy" with cool powers, or the teacher who'll do anything to keep you from failing; he is a hero. He could stop the beating, the torture at any time and yet He doesn't. You see Him decide to keep to this course, and suddenly humility and submitting to God's will seem like the coolest thing one could ever do. I think the heroic aspect of being Catholic, the bravery and charisma it takes to be pro-life and pro-Magisterium, is the kind of thing that attracts young people.

Another thought I have during my classes is that art is about choices. Artists choose one colour over another, one style over another, one composition over another. It is the summing up of those choices in the hands of an artist and his vision that makes a work of art great or not. Life, too, is about choices. Each decision adds to the work of art which is our life, and we should try to make it into a Botticelli, a Michelangelo, or a Memling according to our own vision. The Baroque period is all about this, as are many of the teachings of John Paul II, and I think it has been a powerful force of attraction to the Church. The idea that one is a protagonist has a very strong appeal to young people.

John Lonergan
Governor of Mountjoy Jail

As an institution, the church must become much more vocal and active around social issues. It must openly identify with those in our society who are thought of as the Least, the Last and the Lost. To have real credibility with young people, the Church must not just preach the Gospels, but must live them. The philosophy is the easy part; living it is the real test.

I believe an active caring Church will attract young people to celebrate.

George Lynch
Director, Aid to the Church in Need

We all agree that it is essential to keep the young on board with the faith — why are they falling away?

My first question is: are they being introduced to the faith at home as kids? Are Mam and Dad saying morning or evening prayers with them? Are they being brought to Mass on Sundays? When they start school, what is being taught about the faith?

Children prepare for Holy Communion but after receiving the sacrament, they struggle to remember the Our Father, and the Creed and the Angelus are hardly recited. This is all before secondary school.

While conducting a "Growing in Faith" programme with post-Confirmation teenagers, none believed that the Devil exists or that evil is a reality in the world. Probably the most disappointing thing was that they did not value the faith. How can the young grow in faith if the seeds are not sown? The majority of young people are good, spiritual and charitable but conforming to a strict religious code is not appealing to them. Having to do things as a matter of duty or as a matter of avoiding sin seems alien to them. Where are the answers?

What example are they getting from the bishops, the clergy or their parents? Where can they be reached?

Can they practise without being ridiculed by the media, the trendy or the bullies?

One thing is sure — things must change. Leadership is required to make a start in going back to basics in a modern way. Priests have to become proactive in their parish environment with the help of laity and fight for the attention of the young, making them feel part of the equation.

The one sure thing is that the young are educated and can think and won't accept things because somebody says so.

Fr Owen McCarthy
and Sr Helen Lane
Diocesan Pastoral Renewal Team,
Killarney (Owen) and
School Chaplain (Helen)

In response to your request, we asked a number of
school chaplains and others involved in post-primary
education to forward their responses to your question,
"If you had to suggest one idea which might strengthen
young people's commitment to the Catholic Church,
what would it be?" We also asked a number of those par-
taking in Mater Dei's MA in School Chaplaincy and Pastoral Care to do the same. I'm afraid all I got back was
one response, which you'll find below:

"The single greatest inspiration and challenge that
the Catholic Church could offer young people would be
to engage deeply, openly, authentically and prayerfully
with the issues confronting itself. If the Church did that
they wouldn't have a need to be concerned with marketing or attracting people. The light of truth would draw
people. Young people are great 'sniffers' of the authentic
and the inauthentic. They need to see congruence in an
individual and group. Thus where there are aspects of
the system or attitudes that seem to be at variance with
the spirit of the Gospels, they need to be addressed with
humility. Having an attitude of 'we already know the full

truth' and 'that's not up for discussion' is a major turn-off and quite out of kilter with the questioning spirit of this age. Thus, I reiterate: Engage with openness, authenticity and prayer in the issues facing the Church. Do not be afraid to speak. And trust in the Holy Spirit; not just an idea, but the ultimate creative force!"

Fr Michael McCullagh CM
St Peter's Church, Phibsboro

Thank you so much . . . it is so encouraging to find someone like yourself inviting others into this ministry.

I came in September 2002 and have been gathering young people every week, for Sunday evening liturgy, followed by a meal and often hosting a guest speaker.

OK, one idea . . .

From my reading on ministry to young people and from meeting others I realised that they benefit enormously from "mission" abroad.

I recommend a short period in the first instance from 6 to 10 weeks. It is a way of whetting their appetites and a short acclimatisation time.

If difficulties arise on the part of the hosts or the missionary then there is not such a great problem in such a short time span.

What actually happens?

1. They see a new emerging church and new vocations. (I have been sending them to Ethiopia).

2. They meet poverty face to face and begin to reflect on deeper issues in our world.

3. They encounter a generosity in indigenous workers (many of them teachers) who serve others for little or no remuneration.

4. They begin to reflect on their own personal stories and values and deal with issues that may have lain dormant for some time.

5. Before departing they meet other young people who have been lay volunteers and a mission of like-to-like ensues.

6. On their return they speak of the love and affection they receive from the people.

7. They realise how privileged they are in terms of possessions and possibilities.

8. Often they speak of how their faith is strengthened and deepened.

9. They become involved in their local churches or Christian movements on their return.

10. They have a desire to return again to the mission for a longer term.

Well, that is one idea. It is all new to me and I am only slowly growing it from scratch for myself! The God of surprises is very much there in the young people who come knocking on our doors here.

Brendan McDonald
Actor and TV Continuity Announcer

I'm not sure if I can pinpoint or suggest just *one* thing that would have us all flocking to Church. I reckon I'm fairly representative of your average Irish male when it comes to religion — born and raised Catholic, still have a belief in God (for whatever reason), but never go to Mass — except Christmas Day with the family. I think what's put us "youngsters" off attending regularly is that the Catholic Mass hasn't changed in years and years, and is incredibly formulaic. I can still recite stuff like the Profession of Faith by heart without ever really thinking about what it means, and I reckon I'm not alone there.

The Mass lasts 40 minutes, and only five of that is taken up by the priest's homily, which once every so often can actually mean something to you. I suppose we are all bored by today's Mass, and it seems to have less and less meaning for Ireland's youth — understandably. They have tried to funk it up a bit, I suppose, with the Joys of Folk Mass, but that just means that the Our Father now takes five minutes instead of one!

Perhaps if they concentrated more on a mass that involved less prayer and more of a message of Christianity or Peace, it might make things more appealing: an environment where you were actually interested to hear what a (preferably younger) priest has to say. Basically, there isn't much for people our age to connect with in today's Mass and I suppose the more it stays the same, the more we will stay away.

Not sure if that's any help to you — possibly more of a rant than anything else. I suppose if you look at how much enjoyment people get out of Gospel Masses in the States, and how eager they are to sing along and "Give Praise" — maybe that's something the Church could look at. But we are possibly too set in our ways and just too damn white to let go and start belting out "Praise be to Jesus" at the back of the church. I know I'd be at my local church a lot more often if there were some degree of enjoyment like that.

Anyway, that's my rambling two cents. And remember: no matter what people say or suggest: *nobody knows anything*! Go forth and create.

Dearbhail McDonald
Religious Correspondent with The Sunday Times

I've thought long and hard about this one. It is tricky, as the Church has an unbelievable task ahead of it as it tries to repair the damage caused by the clerical abuse scandals. That debate has raged for the last two decades, and will have influenced a lot of the apathy and mistrust that many young people have of the institutional church. For many of today's teenagers, they will have grown up with only negative media coverage of the Church. Additionally, they may have witnessed their parents' own disillusion too.

I don't think there is one single initiative/idea that would make the church more attractive. There are too many! However, in answer to your question, "If you had to suggest one idea that would make the Church more attractive to young people, what would it be?"

I would say, quite simply: "Listen to them".

Patsy McGarry
*Religious Affairs Correspondent,
The Irish Times*

One idea? Service! Young people are, generally, idealistic. They are also compassionate. And they like to "do" — to be active. That includes today's young. Much derided, as have been the youth of every generation. It was always so.

Let the Church "do" and they will follow. Let it do as the great religious orders did in nineteenth-century Ireland — going into the most deprived and neglected areas of life and dedicating themselves to medically healing, educating, financially helping, lifting the poor out of their squalor.

Those great people not only believed in hope as a Christian virtue, they gave hope too, to those who had nowhere else to turn: through charity, that other great Christian virtue. Both virtues in turn "bred" faith — the last of that blessed Trinity.

Their work also bred a love for members of those religious orders, which persisted until recently. Still does among some. There is, of course, nothing new in this. Look at Francis of Assisi, St Vincent de Paul, Mother Teresa, the St Egidio community, spanning centuries yet doing the same thing. None had/have problems recruiting young followers to the Church/Christ.

Just "do it" and they'll come. The rest will follow.

Fr Peter McVerry SJ
Campaigner for the homeless and founder of the Arrupe Society

The Church affirms the dignity of all human beings as children of God. Nothing can take away or diminish that dignity. Justice seeks to make that dignity a reality in our world and in the lives of those whose dignity has been taken away or undermined by the way in which they are treated by society. Hence, for me, unless the Church is struggling to bring justice to those on the margins of our national societies and our global society, then its preaching that we are all children of God is a sham, a hypocrisy. Hence, I believe that the Church ought to be on the side of those on the margins, supporting their struggle for a rightful place in our society and a fair share of the resources of our planet, being their voice and helping them to articulate their own just demands. In such a scenario, our churches in poor areas would be packed, as the poor would see the Church as their ally, and the churches in middle-class areas would be half-empty, as many would not want to hear what the Church is saying. In reality, it is the other way around, which makes me wonder what we are preaching at all! Such a Church would not sit comfortably in a society like Ireland.

Young people respect and value justice and fairness. If the Church were to pursue such values, at the risk, in-

deed the reality, of losing those who do not want the
Church to make them uncomfortable or challenge the
security of their lives — that is to say, of losing financial
contributions and making the lives of those who preach
the Gospel much poorer and simpler — then young people would respect the Church much more. Instead, the
Church presents to them an institution, comfortably
middle-class, which is firmly integrated into a society
that is unjust, and which fails to challenge that injustice.

Richard Mohan
Prior, Lough Derg

In answer to your question I have to make a distinction between those who are committed and those who are not. Assuming there is commitment I believe that any kind of togetherness, community, belonging to a group of like-minded young people will strengthen the commitment. The support, the encouragement, the craic will keep them bonded and give them encouragement to keep going.

If there isn't commitment to start off with then it's different and can be very difficult.

I believe that if they can be brought in touch with "Church" through some shared experience, probably a challenging one — the more authentic the better (for example a walk or fast or project or retreat or pilgrimage) — they may keep in touch through their peers.

I include an answer from a young man on our staff:

> "To strengthen young people's commitment to the Church, the Church needs to be committed to them, by acknowledging that the future of the Church lies with them, by being responsive to their concerns and needs and ultimately through the realisation that they are the Church."

Aaron Mullaney
Founder, Teen Spirit

The beauty of having Jesus in your life is that He has you and you have Him. There is no stronger bond than that and nothing or nobody can break it. Unfortunately, young people like myself are not given the opportunity of making the best friend they'll ever have — someone to run to when you are scared, to talk to when something is bothering you and to rejoice with when you feel His grace.

If the Church wants the youth of today back in the home of Christ then they'll have to be prepared to re-form. One thing parents should not do is to make their children go to Mass for the sake of it. This instantly creates a problem; when you come to Jesus, you must go freely with an open mind and heart. Only then can you truly embrace God's beauty and presence! Jesus will always be there for you one hundred per cent but he can't and won't be revealed to a hardened heart, and who can blame Him?

Thankfully, my parents gave both my siblings and I the liberty to make our own decisions to attend Church or not. For a time, I was really lost and I stopped going to Church. I realised I was going there to fulfil the wishes of others and not my own. This was totally wrong of me and what's more, it wasn't fair to God! I always knew

God was this mighty and superior power, but I felt I didn't know Him on a personal level — in fact, He was a stranger to me! I no longer wanted it to be this way so I decided to search for God and learn about Him. While at church, I never grasped the true love I now hold for Him. His presence wasn't felt and I just thought it lacked emotion. To be blatantly honest, I just felt numb there!

Then, one March morning, I struggled into school with a big frown on my face. I heard people saying that today was going to be "some doss" because there was a retreat on the whole day. To be honest, I was delighted to learn this and even tried to take advantage of the situation by mitching!

But that didn't go to plan and I am so grateful that's how it turned out. I would have missed out on one of the most joyful and spiritual days of my little life. I would also have missed the opportunity to make a true friend who will always be there for me . . . Jesus! I learned so much more about my amazing friend in that one day than in all the years put together falling asleep at Mass! These young people that spoke of Jesus had such an impact on me that I could honestly feel the love of Christ surrounding my heart!

From that moment on, I have been consumed with happiness having found this blessing in my life. But it is funny to reflect back and to think that I spent all those years at Church and I never captured that special moment with God. I cannot see why the Church is so reluctant to change and to move with the times. "Anchored to the rock . . . geared to the times" is the motto for Youth for Christ, and a very wise outlook it is. Of course, God is the centre as always, but if we want young people to come back to the Church, we need to bring back the passion for Christ that was once there when His amazement was first discovered. And that means walking freely with God, removing the barriers and shining in our lives to inspire the youth.

Ronan Mullen
Commentator and Columnist, The Irish Examiner

I have two suggestions.

Firstly, because I work as a commentator and columnist, I reflect a lot on the media and its relationship with society and the Catholic Church. Many church members feel the media is damaging society. They are at least partly right. While the exposure of scandals has helped to make people more accountable, the corresponding loss of trust in people and institutions is bad news. We are made more cynical about life when other people's failures get disproportionate attention. Where good news is no news, our willingness to learn from each other's wisdom and life experience is lessened.

So we need more constructive media. Shouldn't the Church help provide it? As Christians we need to consider not just what we are going to say to the media in the future, but what kind of media we want to create. Is there any hope of a Church-affiliated foundation charged with the task of investing in ethical print and broadcast media over the next 20 years? Has the Church any plans to use advertising more effectively to communicate its message about life? And will it (we) identify and train lay people to communicate about faith and values in the media, and not just on an ad hoc basis, but in a regular and systematic way?

Imagine the benefits that would accrue from having a national daily newspaper, which reported on all the issues of the day to a very high standard of accuracy and fairness and which also brought the Church's social teaching into the foreground. A resource like that would keep committed Catholics well informed and perhaps attract some non-believers to the Church. But it could also become a centre of ethical, truthful journalism — an example that others might follow.

It goes without saying that an organisation like that won't spring up in the next six months. But are we planning for the day when it might? My sense is that Church leaders know how to manage existing infrastructural and financial resources but are not sufficiently engaged with the task of shaping the evolving culture. Strategic thinking is needed. There are plenty of committed Christians around: people skilled in business, management, communication, advertising, who, if brought on board, could make interesting things happen. Find them. And harness them.

* * *

In the shorter term, why not apply to host World Youth Day in Ireland? At the time of writing, there is talk about a possible Papal visit. I think such an event would be a great success, a moment of reconciliation perhaps, and that the turnout would be much greater than the sceptics think.

However, to maximise the potential for evangelising youth, this papal visit should coincide with the Church's annual World Youth Day.

I was in Rome for World Youth Day in the Jubilee Year of 2000 along with about 2,000 young people from Ireland. There was something very thought-provoking and inspiring about the sight of thousands of young people, from all parts of the world, coming together to pray, reflect and celebrate with their mentor in the faith. The display of diversity of race, socio-economic background, temperament, style and spirituality was impressive. And the good humour, the sheer graciousness of people, was an advertisement for Christian faith.

Why shouldn't this happen in Ireland? Hundreds of thousands of young people coming to Ireland. Learning about our Christian heritage. And teaching us something of their own.

We've had the Special Olympics. This would be another great celebration of life.

Bríd Ní Rinn
Ecclesiastical Sculptress

My answer is that they must be able to understand and explain their faith. Since 1962, Christian doctrine has not been properly taught in schools. Young people, I think, are quite tough enough to understand full and orthodox Catholic doctrine, and they do not need a watered-down version such as is taught to children. At the very least, everyone should have a copy of the Catechism of the Catholic Church. Being a Catholic is a public matter — it is not a secret society or cult.

As to activities, young people would be good at reviving old pilgrimages . . . with proper praying and not Pagan or New Age rituals. Young people need to be warned, I think, about Heaven and Hell and sin and the Devil, because there are some present-day practices, such as psychic sessions or use of tarot cards, which are dangerous. My main idea, however, is that young people should take up the study, teaching and promotion of the faith. Youth can do it!

Breda O'Brien
Columnist, The Irish Times

I believe young people need to experience people and places where living the Christian message is a source of challenge, joy and fulfilment. Many young people have only experienced the barest remnant of cultural Catholicism, and have never seen a vibrant Christian community in action.

We adults need to be convinced of the value of what we have been given ourselves. In however flawed and human a way, we need to model an alternative to the sometimes mindless consumerism which is being peddled today.

Judy O'Brien
Assistant Co-ordinator,
Daughters of Charity, Holy Angels

I think young people see the church as a place that they are dragged out of their beds to on a Sunday morning, to sit in the cold and listen to usually a long-winded sermon or a letter from the bishop that is of no interest to them. So they have nothing stored that would encourage them to return. So I think that the Church has a lot of work to do to restore that.

They have got to hit them where they find them, in front of the telly: documentaries with involvement from youth production teams, being seen in the community as real people, as part of the community and not set apart in parochial houses, or as wealthy property owners. They could canvass, as they did in the past. They could try it with a new slant, not as Bible thumpers. They could work in paid employment, marry or not as they so choose, join the local clubs, fitness, night classes, set-dancing, etc.

In other words, do what "real people" do!

Fr Martin O'Connor LC
Legionaries

My idea is the following. This is pre-evangelisation work:

1. Create an open forum for discussion for the young people (age 16–30). For under-18s, the tough question is just how to make this happen.

2. For older age groups, there is an apostolate that has worked well in the US and has had some successful pilot programmes in Dublin called "Theology on Tap" (age 20+), meeting on a Tuesday or Wednesday night in a good clean atmosphere, a pub of good repute, one speaker on topics of general spiritual interest, i.e. "Why do we suffer", "Does God Exist?", "Was Christ God?", "Good and Evil, Heaven and Hell"; after the talk, questions and answers and a pint. The feedback has been excellent.

Once the seed is sown with the young people, their journey back to the Church is rather short.

They need their questions answered with clarity and conviction. The problem is finding the people with the conviction to stand up and take them on. Once this happens, faith becomes logical to them. Our faith is very reasonable!

I think it is important to say where I want to go with this idea. I am not promoting the "drink" scene at all. I simply think it is important to "reach" the young people where they are at . . . offer them a venue and a chance to speak their mind on spiritual issues and to get answers that are challenging, as the Gospel is. Young people want a challenge. Our materialistic-hedonistic world is just too easy for them.

How this is to be done is precisely the question but it needs to be done *much* more effectively on all levels, 12–14, 15–17, 18–23, 25+, according to their stage of maturity.

Raymond O'Connor
Pioneer and Total Abstinence Association

The Church should simply preach the truth and be faithful to it and not be afraid of the adverse reaction it will receive. They will always receive negative publicity — that's par for the course. However, I believe in the long term that people will realise that maybe the Church was not wrong after all in its teachings on divorce, abortion, family planning, sex before marriage, homosexuality, celibacy, etc — teachings which young people find dated and difficult to accept. But that may take a lifetime of course!! The difficulty is that these positions are not explained in a simple, clear manner in the media. We need to change that. Unfortunately, the reality is that young people are no longer attending Mass in large numbers and even at that, the Church rarely speaks out on these issues from the pulpit.

At the end of the day, the media dictates the lifestyle choices of people so perhaps it's time we had knowledgeable Catholic lay people or priests to address these issues in the print media, radio, television, internet and be seen! These issues are the stumbling blocks for many young people today, and unless they're properly addressed, young people will continue to stay away.

I am not saying here that the Church should change its position but should be proactive in educating people as to why it holds a particular viewpoint, mindful of the fact that its duty is to preach the truth, and to uphold that truth.

That's just something I feel the Church needs to do and perhaps it will help the Irish Church to grow again.

Treacy O'Connor
Reiki Master, Dublin

The Church has a lot of questions to answer in my view. I believe they exist only to control their congregations. They have taken people's spiritual power away from them, making us believe that we can only communicate with God through them. This is not true. We all have instant access to God by going within ourselves. A radical change they could make would be to understand this and encourage people to become aware of it, whilst being *spiritual guides* for us, rather than preaching to us and threatening us with the "fear of God".

In the Church's fear of losing valuable customers, they have over the centuries created a false sense of security in all of us. It is not right. People are waking up and searching for the truth. It is time for big change. And it's time for us all to stand in our own truths.

Sr Josepha O'Donnell
Presentation Sisters, Retired Religious Teacher

How wonderful to read your letter in the *Irish Catholic* telling us that you were passionate about the future of your faith and your request for suggestions as to how the Catholic Church can keep its young members interested and active.

My one big suggestion is to reverence the Blessed Sacrament.

Solid doctrine needs to be taught today . . . if we get that right we can build our faith.

As a teacher, my policy was to make sure that my students knew the fundamentals of each subject. If they knew the basics I could build on that. It's the same with the fundamentals of our faith. Get the basics right and we can build a solid true faith.

Fr Silvester O'Flynn OFM Cap
Director of Retreats and Author of Gather in my Name *and "The Good News" Series*

No one idea in particular came to me in answer to your question. So I will respond in a more general way.

Take Acts 2:42, which tells of the four pillars of the early Christian community:

- Faithful to the teaching of the apostles; study of religion

- To the brotherhood: experience of Christ in community, fellowship, caring, charity etc.

- To the breaking of bread: understanding the Eucharist, good celebration of liturgy.

- To the prayers: in personal prayer, experiences of God's presence, prayer group, psalms etc.

I see these four points like stations on a rail track. One can get on the train at any one of them. In deepening one's commitment to any one of these ways, one gradually grows in the experience of the other three qualities.

Most Rev Leo O'Reilly
Bishop of Kilmore

The diocese of Kilmore where I am bishop is relatively small and rural — about 50,000 Catholics in five counties, mainly Cavan, Leitrim and Fermanagh. The largest town, Cavan, has a population of less than 10,000. We are fortunate to have a very active youth ministry in the diocese, with a priest and a sister working full time with young people. Among the many projects they undertake are school retreats, "Faith Friends" programmes with young people preparing for First Communion and Confirmation, and "Gift" programmes for students at second level. The common element in all these programmes is that young people themselves are trained to minister to their peers (or to those a little younger than them). This has proved to be a very effective way of communicating the Christian message to young people in schools, in parishes and elsewhere. The fact that it is people only a few years older than themselves who are speaking or sharing their experience of faith makes the message much more convincing and more acceptable to the listeners. The participants identify much more readily with a boy or a girl just a few years older than they would with an adult, or with a priest who might be seen as remote from their experience or part of an impersonal institution.

However, as well as being a more effective way of communicating the faith to others, experience has shown that the young people involved as "faith friends" or as members of a retreat team or a pilgrimage team deepen their own faith and commitment greatly. In the training and preparation for presenting the different programmes the young adults begin to learn about their faith and discuss it in depth, perhaps for the first time. They realise they may have to answer questions about their own faith and so they begin to ask questions and search for answers which are personally satisfying to them. As part of the preparation for delivering programmes, they get opportunities to reflect and pray. Prayer is an integral part of all these programmes, so they get into the habit of praying in different ways. Prayer becomes part of their lives, not as a duty to fulfil, and not just as a last resort when all fruit fails, but rather as the expression of a felt need in their lives. It becomes an oasis in their days where they meet Christ and come to know him as a real person. Their religion ceases to be tainted by superstitions or to be a matter of performing rituals, but becomes instead the expression of a personal relationship with Jesus Christ.

So the one idea I would suggest — not so much I have to confess from my own experience as from the experience of those who work with young people in our diocese — is *involvement in mission*. As one who spent a good many years teaching at second level, I realise that you never really learn a subject until you have taught it. The same applies here. Get young people involved in ministry. Empower them to bring the message of Jesus to others of their own age or younger. In doing that, they will appreciate that message in an altogether new way. It will deepen their own conviction and their commitment as well as sharing that faith with others. It will give them a new understanding of their faith and a new enthusiasm for sharing it with others.

Vicky Rattigan

National Development Worker, Young Christian Workers National Office

I spoke to members of our IMPACT! group, both of who have recently turned 18. I put your question to them. Their responses were quite simple: "Make young people feel welcome." This was followed by the usual statements made by many these days that "the Mass should be related more to people's lives" and that "the Gospel message is not getting out there" and therefore not being applied. Both young people said that there was a lack of understanding among young people (and others) about their religion.

People often ask me how or why I got involved in YCW. The simple answer to this question is, I was asked. I was working in an office, a difficult enough job. One evening walking home from work I met a former teacher from school, who having long since retired from teaching was doing a stint as the Parish Sister. She stopped me in the street and simply invited me along to a chat about "youth" in the presbytery. Not being a "church-goer" at the time, I reluctantly agreed and went home to ask my mother where the presbytery was.

As agreed, I attended the meeting, which was also attended by a number of others — some the same age as myself, some older, others who like me had been invited to come along and hear what a group of young people from YCW had to say. It was during this meeting that I found out what the initials "YCW" actually stood for. As someone who had absolutely no contact with parish, church or any other form of religious practice, you can imagine how the C part of Young Christian Workers struck me. "Here come the Bible bashers," I thought to myself and kept a close eye on my watch ready with my excuse to bolt out the door as soon as I could. The lecture didn't come. What I did hear was a group of young people talking about the things that they felt strongly about, the things that were important to them. Work, unemployment, life and other social issues were being discussed and acted on by these young people who were just like me. There was nothing earth-shattering about that first encounter with YCW but I did agree to come back the following week to what was to become Francis Street YCW's first meeting.

No matter what the group or organisation, people join things for many different reasons. Why they stay, however, is what's really important. I joined YCW because I was invited to do so. The reasons I stayed were many and varied. I wouldn't say I was actually searching for something; I had a job, friends and a good social life. As far as I was concerned there was nothing missing in my life. Looking back on my time in the movement, I realise that what I actually found was a place where I could belong. Being part of a group of my peers where what I said really mattered was one thing, but being part of an International Movement which offered opportunities to travel was quite another story altogether. In our group in Francis Street, we looked at different issues, situations which we as young people were facing every day of the week. Using the YCW method of "See, Judge, Act" we looked at each situation, reflected on it and took actions that made a real difference in our own lives and the lives of those around us. This same method was changing the lives of thousands of other young workers throughout the world.

For me, I know that had I not joined YCW, I would have long since joined my peers in their exodus from the Church. There are many different groups and organisations working with young people today. Some are issue-based, others more spiritual in their approach. YCW worked for me because it combined everything: from the physical, spiritual and emotional aspects to the very practical everyday things like knowing your rights and entitlements. I have met many young people throughout Europe who have been changed by this movement — young people with a true sense of their own worth and of their ability to bring about change in the workplace, in society but most importantly in their Church.

For me, Church is more than a building, going to Mass etc. It's about community and living out your faith in the everyday things in life. YCW provided the opportunity for me to do just that. Many other organisations do similar work but what is really important is that young people are invited to participate and given every opportunity to make a real contribution to the life of the Church.

Young people are our future but they are also our present. I don't have any specific answers to your question other than to say, invite young people to participate in Church, meet them where they are at and give them a positive experience.

As Cardijn himself said: "We are only at the beginning, at the very beginning. We must persevere."

Marc Sheridan
Marketing Brand Manager with Pulse Group, formerly of Guinness

Interestingly, this is what jumped into my mind: a previous Marketing Manager in Guinness identified the "lack of recruitment" to the Church as a reflection of the "lack of recruitment" to the Guinness brand. Hence, the brief was about tackling one to understand the other.

The key insight was quite simple considering the amount of time/research/energy that went into the question . . .

Youth are now tribal. They operate within their own groupings and a hierarchy within the group is established — a tribe with leaders, followers, providers, clowns, etc. The tribe hierarchy is affected by how you speak, what you speak about, what you wear, what you eat, drink, etc. Brands (let's consider the Church a brand — which it is) have a very fine line to play with; if they step either side of that line they either miss (1) relevance or (2) credibility. If you get it right, you become "accepted" within their tribe/group — but not for long, as you need to change with their needs to remain relevant/credible.

I think (1) relevance and (2) credibility are two primary issues facing the Church brand. There is no longer relevance to young people's lives. Like an old brand which hasn't kept pace with change, youth can rebel: "well if you're not willing to meet my needs, my trends (respect me) then why should I bother with you?" Credibility is a far more serious issue to address in light of the continual and some would feel still unknown level of child abuse and corruption.

Hence your idea needs to address these two core issues. There is light at the end of the tunnel, however. There is a growing search for "truth and simplicity" among youth and a need to belong. Only if the brand can address the second issue first, can it start to build relevance.

Hence, my thought is that people/youth *want* to believe, need to belong, and are looking for truth and simplicity.

Fr Jim Stanley CSsR
Director of Vocations Ireland

My one suggestion is: "invite and engage them in any worthwhile project that involves service and giving" — not just talking, discussion, thinking and praying, important as all these are. When we begin to serve and to do, things happen. God responds and in the giving, we receive and the kingdom of God begins to grow. Young people are as generous and idealistic today as ever, despite all the selfishness and materialism that abound. In engaging them we are actually doing them a favour.

Alice Taylor
Writer

We need more of the joy of music and singing in our churches. The entire congregation singing! People feel good after singing. Jesus said, "The truth will set you free."

We need to feel the freedom. If we depress ourselves in Church, we are losing the essence of the divine message. So let's hear the music and the song!

Alice Taylor's niece, Marie Taylor, writes:

I think there should be more discussion between members. People could try to help each other solve problems, and learn from listening to each other. People communicate on such a superficial level in their day-to-day lives and also when they go to Church it's all a bit impersonal. People carry around so many worries and pain; I think the Church should be helping people to help themselves.

Fr John Wall PP
Clondalkin Parish

I have been working with young adults since we started the "Ballyfermot Peace Corps" way back in 1972, when I had all my hair! It has since developed and is now called the "Localise" movement with its office in Rathmines.

The attraction of young people to "caring in the community", i.e. action, is still working, thank God. We'll be out around Clondalkin tomorrow (in fancy dress!) collecting for People in Need.

Faith *and* good works seems to be the combination.

The dropout or opt-out phenomenon that perennially affected young people in their transition to maturity has become even more pertinent today in the post-Confirmation youngster's commitment to Church.

To a young person, it is a sign of growing up that "whatever you were before" you are no longer now! Opting out of liturgical practice is almost a sign of growing up.

Peer pressure is underpinned by genuine grievances. The Church's image as a killjoy — especially in the powerful arena of the passions — doesn't make it a desirable place for a teenager or young adult to be. Then there are the puzzling mind-shifts entailed in growing up. For a child, belief in the existence of God and belief in the existence of, say, France, come under the same category of "knowledge" or "fact". It's "stuff I've learned". As a young person grows up, the difference between truth of fact and truth of faith becomes very marked.

Now, to assist a young person in the transition from a child's "knowledge" to an adult faith requires a lot of *accompaniment*.

The best form of accompaniment, in my opinion, is provided in the context of what we might call an "ecclesial" experience — a feeling of *belonging* to a peer group that respects me and yet challenges me to achieve really good ideals, where talent is tapped and confidence is encouraged.

The approach, so, is not directly catechetical; it is contextual. Theologically speaking, it is a smallish community where Gospel values are experienced.

It is in this context that faith and "church" questions arise and a reason for worship may be rediscovered by the budding young mind. This can be done chiefly through the experience of meditation on, for example, the wonder of creation, the beauty of human life or even on flawed humanity, and through pilgrimages or outings to places of Christian culture.

The actual provision of such an accompaniment and ecclesial experience is the obvious difficulty. My own practical experience in this regard mostly revolves around working with young people in "Localise". Young people come together under the banner of "Caring in the Community". It is not specifically church-based so "seekers-after-truth" feel comfortable. It's "Okay not to be okay", as the phrase has it. The ecclesial feeling comes from the caring for each other and from working out of a Gospel-value base of justice and of caring for the un-cared-for.

This sort of action-experience appeals to many young people. But there are other possibilities, depending on the personal choices and talents of the young person. For those who have interest in political change, there is YCW. There are Gospel Choirs and in Dublin there are many specifically Faith/Evangelisation programmes available from the diocesan Catholic Youth Care. But there is no copyright on common sense. Any group that provides accompaniment to young people, in the context of basic Gospel values, will, in my experience, allow the Spirit to take root and a young church to flower.

Most Rev Willie Walsh DD
Bishop of Killaloe

I would prefer to think how we might attract young people to Christ — all the baptised, young or old, already
belong to the Church. I believe that the only effective
way to attract people to Christ is to try to live our lives
trying to follow the example and teaching of Christ.
Young people will not be impressed by what we say or
preach. They will be influenced by the way they see us
living our lives.

Selected Responses from Other Contributors

Justin Barrett, Mother and Child Campaign

"Give them the truth: *Veritas*."

Cait Breathnach, County Wicklow

"My answer is music. Young people (and not so young people) are moved, often passionately, by music. Music performers have become their heroes, for better or worse."

Moya Brennan, Singer, formerly of Clannad

"Involve them, make them feel part of what's going on and let them do things which have meaning to them."

Philomena Burns

"I think we must give the young people today what they are familiar with. The main thing they like is music. I think the film *Sister Act* showed this very clearly. When Whoopi Goldberg took over the choir in the convent in which she was hiding, the youngsters who lounged around the streets flocked in."

Fr Jim Caffrey, Director, Catholic Youth Care

"I would love to see young people reading the Gospels using the method of *Lectio Divina*. The Gospels have the power to change their lives and by falling in love with Jesus Christ they will in turn reach out to the poor and needy. The starting point is to help them open the Bible and read the Gospel."

Rev Paul Clayton-Lea, Teacher, St Patrick's Grammar School, Armagh

"Attracting young people to the Church is of course a multi-faceted exercise! As you ask for just one idea then I have to boil it down to saying that if we want to attract young people to the church then we have to acknowledge their presence more openly among us and try to address some of their concerns as well as offer them ideals by which to live."

Rachel Collier, Developer and Manager of Young Social Innovators (YSI)

"I think the church needs to speak with and to young people more. It is one of my frequent thoughts! I also think it is pertinent for YSI, as social awareness education and social responsibility and citizenship is what the church needs to be involved in more at the action level."

Winnifred Collins

"I would suggest the attention should first be paid to reaching out to the young men in each parish. Women have taken over everything now, and I think men need to be brought together, something like the Men's Sodalities, which used to take place, where they could be taught their faith and up-to-date issues covered from a Catholic point of view. Where fathers could attend with their sons and the sons got a feeling of maturity and masculinity."

John Costello, Apple Computers, Cork City

"I have a thing about long and boring sermons. Leave out sermons; I have rarely heard a sermon that grabs my attention. Most people have a short attention span and if the sermon needs to grab you in the first 30 seconds or else sermons should be short and relevant to today's world."

Dylan Cotter, Irish International Advertising

"That in the face of sense and science, the Church . . . presents religion for what it really is: a metaphorical instruction booklet for sharing a planet with a few billion other people without killing any of them."

Marjorie Cunniam

"I personally think that they need to get the true teaching of the Ten Commandments to understand the beauty of the Catholic Church."

Monsignor Brendan Devlin, Maynooth College

"Transmission of faith to family and friends."

Michael Egan, County Roscommon

"From my brief experience (I am 19) of parish priests in my area, I have noted that when there is a relatively young (25–55 years) and active priest in the parish, the youth become more involved and more willing to participate in activities both within and outside the Church. As a result, morale within the parish is high."

Elizabeth Flaherty, County Limerick

"Sadly, the Mass is not understood sufficiently by most people, and certainly not by the young. Catholic children are not being taught their Catholic Faith. The Ten Commandments have been dumped and wishy-washy Catechetics is a poor substitute at best and misleading at worst: sometimes, a mixture of religions, ending in confusion and inability to distinguish between right and wrong."

Louisa Glennon, DIT Graduate and Researcher

"Here's my contribution. It's the summary of a college assignment I did on why young people don't go to Mass and how to get them back, so it's probably relevant! Eight ideas:

1. Give young people's opinions an airing

2. Make Mass times more accessible

3. Revive Stations of the Cross

4. Re-educate young and middle-aged priests
5. Make Catholicism a Leaving Cert subject
6. Make religious movies part of curriculum
7. Celebrity endorsement of Mass
8. Youth role models."

Sr Una Kearney, Director of Contemplative Retreats for 18–36-year-olds

"To encounter a witness who is living the Gospel with joy within the Church community is the greatest incentive to commitment for a young person. Any retreats or meetings facilitating such an encounter is the idea I suggest."

Ide Kiely, "a religious engaged in work with youth"

"I am sending you a one-liner: A growing personal relationship with Jesus Christ: i.e. explore the Gospels!"

Justin Kilcullen, Director of Trocaire

"A radical reform of the Sunday liturgy to make it relevant, interesting and attractive to young people. The development of a comprehensive Youth Ministry within the Church."

Gertie McEnroe, County Longford

"Re Baptism: parents and godparents should have serious instruction on their duties; if they're not practising, there's little chance for the child."

Gerald McKeon

"A central agency dealing with young Catholics' spirituality: promote this throughout schools, youth clubs, churches, etc. Basically, something to which young people can turn for advice on starting on their spiritual journey and where they can go to develop it/explore it e.g. Youth 2000. Many young people would be shy about approaching a local priest."

Noreen McKeone

"I would like to see Sunday school for young kids being introduced. This would help kids to become familiar with the Bible and give them a good moral understanding. Also, for older kids, something like the Church of Ireland Ventures would be of benefit. It would help them to make friends and socialise with like-minded people. Alpha courses geared towards younger people have proved to be very effective in educating our young people in the basics of Christianity."

Sister M. Baptist Meany, Presentation Sisters, Cork

"Try to set up small Christian communities."

Fr Gerard Moloney CSsR, Editor, *Face Up* Magazine and Redemptorist Preacher

"If we want to attract young to the Church, I think we have got to look at the quality of our liturgies. Liturgies in this country tend to be very poor. They do not connect with the young. Parishes must invest in good quality liturgy as a matter of urgency."

Sr M. de Sales Murphy, Teacher, School Principal, Local Superior and Superior General, Ursuline Sisters, in Ireland, USA and Kenya

"I've only got one deep conviction: what our troubled Church today needs above all is people totally involved in a deep and loving relationship with God. Even one person, irrespective of status — clergy, laity, married, single — in such a deep relationship is an uplift to the Church and exercises an influence on others."

Cliona Ní Ghiolla, Belfast

"Youth are responding well to Justice and Charity, and it was wonderful to see the Belvedere lads fasting and sleeping rough for the week over Christmas. Listen to them and get them to write their own needs and how they see the future."

John D. Nugent, "lapsed Catholic", County Roscommon

"Who, amongst them, wants to strengthen their commitment to the Church — of all things? But most of them have time for God and you would be surprised at how many actually pray most sincerely. If the young people could be got to strengthen their commitment *to God*, I think you might get places with them."

Sister Malachy O'Farrell, St Clare's Convent, Dublin

"I suggest membership of the following groups: The Legion of Mary. Youth 2000 has branches all over."

Janet O'Connor, Church of Ireland

"I feel that to make young people more interested in the Church and to strengthen their commitment in the Church of Ireland, one would have to give them more ownership over it. It's almost like the majority of people who go to church are old and they are there because they want to cleanse their souls before they die so they go to heaven. I know from my own experience that I, along with my two sisters and brother, was dragged there every Sunday against my will. I know as well, that if I have kids I will probably drag them to church like my parents did to us. It did make us feel like we belonged to something — whereas my atheist friends in primary school didn't have any sense of belonging to a community."

Sean O'Farrell

"The home, the domestic Church is crucial. Not only must parents pass on and teach their faith to their children, they must live it to the full and encourage their offspring to do the same. To begin to do this, there must be an atmosphere of prayer in the home."

Lorcain Ó hAlmhain, Isle of Man

"The one idea that I would suggest to attract young people to the Church is to set up some framework or activity to inform these people what they ought to do to be a part of the Church. Clearly demonstrate what role they can play within the Church. Too often, younger people are turned away from the Church by being told that the only thing available is the 'folk group'."

Gillian O'Sullivan, Teacher and Olympic Athlete

"If the Church could concentrate on getting young people to understand the relevance of the Church to their lives — this could be done by using examples from the life of Jesus and comparing with modern living. The focus point should be that the moral values of goodness, honesty and kindness are still relevant and important in modern-day situations."

Ruth O'Sullivan, County Cork

"Of course, for many, if not all activities, a church hall is a necessity. I was surprised when I moved here to find that there was no hall attached to the church."

Seán O'Sullivan, County Cork

"Young married people and those in new houses should be encouraged to get their houses blessed and consecrated.

Our mature clergy should regularly undergo refresher courses on how to sell themselves and put 'the message' in a modern way — to meet modern demands and needs and to make it relevant. A bit of zeal and enthusiasm would be a breath of fresh air.

Prayer groups should be in all parishes and clergy should not be reluctant to act as spiritual directors."

Jack Scannell, Legion of Mary, International Toastmasters

"I am nearly 82, and growing up before the last war, we were inspired by wonderful preachers who told us about the various saints. I can still hear vividly what they said. Sadly, this type of sermon is gone, and I see no hope of attracting a new generation into our Church until we get back those priests who can speak."

Lee Sorenson, Communion and Liberation

"It would be difficult to put into words how to attract young people to the church. The method that I would use would be to accompany them, showing them my happiness and positivity and thereby awakening in them a curiosity as to the source of this happiness: thus the church."

Brendan Tarrant

"Many of the problems in the world today stem from materialism, in short, from the adoration of false gods. If we remove the false gods from our own lives, we will then be able to focus more on the true God and make room for Him to come into our own lives. Then, when young people see our faith in action, they will be encouraged to follow and our words will not be hypocritical."

Fr Martin Tierney PP, *The Irish Catholic*

"To strengthen commitment within the Church, I would encourage young people already committed to Christ to witness to their faith without fear."

"Young Person", County Kerry

"Start promoting charity work more to younger people. Teach them the rewards of giving."

Part 2

A NEW 95 THESES

Centuries ago, a young German's 95 theses sparked the Reformation. This section suggests reform in a more modest, if perhaps more constructive manner, via 95 theses which were largely derived from the contributions listed in Part 1. These "new 95 theses" have also been inspired by contributions which were either edited or left out of Part 1 due to space considerations or overall lack of direct context. Some theses were not specifically recommended, but were alluded to by contributors or listed because of what some contributors have themselves done (e.g. setting up a political party). Finally, a number of ideas were included by the author as potential modules of a Leaving Certificate syllabus: this was a development of a core thesis which suggested Catholicism as a Leaving Certificate subject.

Thus, Part 2 serves as a bridge between all contributions to this project and the survey presented in Part 3. It summarises the arguments of Part 1, adds some further voices to the debate and serves up the questionnaire which provides this book's real reformational potential.

For the purposes of the resultant school question-naire, the wording of these theses has been adapted to be as comprehensible and apt as possible. Some ideas like "alpha groups" and "Lectio Divina" that were either very specific or not familiar to all likely participants were pre-sented in a simpler format, e.g. "attendance of retreats" or "reading of the Gospels".

These "new 95 theses" are outlined below, in the or-der in which they appeared on the school questionnaire. This order was determined firstly by the thesis length, and then by theme. Where appropriate, the thesis is jus-tified and/or supported by relevant quotations.

#1

Invite young people to air their views and listen to them

About one in five respondents mentioned this idea. In fact, it was the most cited of the 95 presented:

"People in this Church need to be real, authentic, honest and involved in a deep relationship with Christ, while walking the journey with people, listening to their stories" — Fr Harry Bohan.

"Get the young people together and ask them what can I do to help them." — Fr Hugh Hanley.

"I do think the Church needs to speak with and to young people more." — Rachel Collier.

"What I did hear was a group of young people talking about the things that they felt strongly about, the things that were important to them." — Vicky Rattigan on what attracted her to YCW at first.

"People could try to help each other solve problems and learn from listening to each other." — Marie Taylor.

"I would, quite simply, listen to them." — Dearbhail McDonald.

"It would be good to get young people together for a good, loud, heated debate . . . make sure that everyone feels able to talk openly . . . the most important thing is that young people are consulted." — Rebecca Leavy.

"The church needs to be more passive rather than aggressive in its approach to young people and needs to listen rather than judge." — Vanessa Conneely.

"The Church needs to find ways of listening to the voice of young people, of forming partnerships with them, if it is to be relevant now and in the future." — Sr Stanislaus Kennedy.

With typical proactivity, Fr Brian D'Arcy put this into practice and asked young people himself. "My suggestion," he says, "would be to ask young people themselves. Having asked them I would try to do what they suggested."

#2

Present religion as a roadmap for peace in the world

How many times, especially on this island, have we heard religion being blamed for conflict? The recent bloodshed in Afghanistan and Iraq — and its presentation by some as a war against Islam — has only entrenched such views in a global context. Is there a perception out there that confrontation and war are part and parcel of religion? Conversely, is there an adequate perception among young people about the intrinsically peaceful tenets of the main world religions? Scope indeed, perhaps, for heeding advertising guru Dylan Cotter's advice and focus more on presenting "religion for what it really is: a metaphorical instruction booklet for sharing a planet with a few billion other people without killing any of them".

#3

The Church should be more active in local community

Following an era of concerted pressure to separate Church from State and from virtually everything else, it is interesting to hear several respondents calling for greater Church involvement in their communities! Rebecca Leavy tells us "maybe the clergy need to be more involved in community activities". This is a call echoed by Sister Agnes Haverty in saying, "the Church which appeals to young people is the Church that moves out to meet the people instead of waiting for the people to come". George Lynch sums up both responses when he says, "Priests have to become proactive in their parish environment with the help of laity and fight for the attention of the young, making them feel part of the equation".

#4

Set up small Christian support groups (3–12) for young people

In the Church of tomorrow, might small be the new big? There is certainly a perception that the experience of Mass in our large churches "is all a bit impersonal" (Marie Taylor). The personal touch, via the "experience of Christ in community" that Silvester O'Flynn encourages may be provided if we, as Sister M. Baptist Meany urges, "try to set up small Christian communities". Indeed, Karl Rahmer predicted that the Church of the future will be one built from below by basic communities. Monsignor Patrick Devine's opinion was that "the new challenges that come in early teens seem to require an appropriate social support group with which the over-13s can identify, and in which this initial goodwill can be fostered and matured".

As if to illustrate that progress has already been made, the Appendix provides details of a number of innovations in this area. Concepts such as Fr Michael Hurley's "Cell Groups" and the Presentation communities' "Communio" idea may indeed be the shape of "the Church of the future". After all, who was it that said, "where two or three are gathered in my name, there am I in the midst of them" (*Matthew 18:20*)?

#5

Change Mass dramatically for young people

If, as Brendan McDonald says, "we are all bored by today's Mass, and it seems to have less and less meaning for Ireland's youth", some changes are surely due? Justin Kilcullen urges "a radical reform of the Sunday liturgy to make it relevant, interesting and attractive to young people".

Gerard Moloney of the Redemptorists makes a similar plea: "If we want to attract young to the Church, I think we have got to look at the quality of our liturgies. Liturgies in this country tend to be very poor. They do not connect with the young. Parishes must invest in good quality liturgy as a matter of urgency."

But where would one start? By allowing young people to air their views, some remedies may become evident. But there is, of course, the distinct possibility that the real symptoms of boredom exist outside the Church building. All roads may, instead, lead to Thesis #56, as Elizabeth Flaherty maintains: "Sadly, the Mass is not understood sufficiently by most people, and certainly not by the young."

#6

Encourage happy vibe at Mass through up-tempo liturgy

On my one encounter at a Born Again Christian service, I was impressed by the congregation's cheerfulness. Thus,

I was not surprised to see Born Again contributor Kevin Brennan say, "young people should be told to give thanks and praise when in Church and be happy". In a similar vein, Sean O'Sullivan agreed, "a bit of zeal and enthusiasm would be a breath of fresh air".

#7

Less prayer and more of a message at Mass

There is also a case to be made — and it's made very well by Brendan McDonald in this book — that there's a distinct lack of mental stimulation at Mass. "I think what's put us youngsters off," he says, "is that the Catholic Mass hasn't changed in years and years, and is incredibly formulaic. I can still recite stuff like the Profession of Faith by heart without ever really thinking about what it means, and I reckon I'm not alone there. The Mass lasts about 40 minutes, and only five of that is taken up by the priest's homily, which every so often can actually mean something to you."

Rather contradictory to some anti-sermon views, Brendan concludes, "if they concentrated more on a Mass that involved less prayer and more of a message of Christianity or Peace, it might make things more appealing".

#8

Have lots more singing at Mass and get everyone singing

As a Catholic who purposefully avoids most Masses involving song, I'm probably not qualified to present this paragraph, but some contributors are so enthusiastic about this topic they speak (or nearly sing) for themselves! I was particularly interested in choirmaster Regina Deacy's thoughts, because she implied that "through singing the Word and attending Mass regularly, [youth] are becoming committed. They are even raising issues and asking questions about things." A very vivid and colourful response came from Philomena Burns, who declared, "the main thing young people like is music":

"I think the film *Sister Act* showed this very clearly when Whoopi Goldberg took over the choir in the convent in which she was hiding, the youngsters who lounged around the streets flocked in."

There's a growing popularity for gospel choirs, though whether this can "get the whole congregation singing" as Alice Taylor recommends is not certain. As one quotation suggests, "we are possibly too set in our ways and just too damn white to let go and start belting out 'Praise be to Jesus' at the back of the Church".

Still, a generation reared on hip-hop, R'n'B, rap and even Gospel may just change that!

#9

Ensure there is a time for personal prayer and quiet reflection at Mass

If the local Mass is one's only meaningful contact with God, can one rely on the "personal prayer" and "experience of God's presence" which Silvester O'Flynn considers so vital, amid the din of screaming babies, kids on constant walkabout and distracted parents? Speaking of the world of inner-city youth, "which is often cluttered with noise", Martin Byrne wishes that "Jesus' Church would gift these youngsters with tools for reflection" and "oases of silence". Indeed, if "prayer" can be, on its own, the single-word answer to this book's central question (as it was for Inishbofin artist and poet Marie Coyne), surely every Mass ought to provide an oasis of calm?

#10

Have a short and motivational sermon

When an ex-International Toastmaster (Jack Scannell) contends that the "wonderful" pre-war standard of preaching "is gone", and an ex-priest (Michael Breen) says modern preaching is "mostly abysmal", "often heretical", "commonly ignorant of the Gospel" and "rarely Christocentric" — and they're the over-30s — you know improvements are due! If motivation is required for young people at Mass, it can't suffice to preach "in a limp fashion with no emphasis" as one contributor put it. Despite this, my local priest delivers wonderfully entertaining sermons, as do seemingly all Redemptorists and clergy and religious I've encountered on Bachelors' Walk and Merchants' Quay. If the talent exists, perhaps a conference, where the highest-rated speakers (by polls of their parishioners) gave tips might work?

#11

Men don't like singing — have specific things at Mass aimed at men

Writing in the *Irish Catholic* (20 November 2003), Mary Kenny remarks, "the people most alienated from faith are men — particularly young men between the ages of 18 and 35". "This", she continues, "is the group least well represented in church attendance."

In one of the most memorable quotes in Part 1, Brendan McDonald, a member of the "Men, 18–34" demographic, refers sarcastically to "the Joys of Folk Mass". The "Folk Mass" — or the mass with a lot of singing — has been a curious attempt to attract young people to the Church in recent times. Indeed, some would argue that it has been the most obvious attempt to do so in the last decade. However, where do men stand in relation to singing — traditionally a practice which finds greater support among women? Brendan claims "it just means that the Our Father now takes five minutes instead of one!" As a male who loves music, and is part of the 18–34 age group, I must concur with both viewpoints. Of the new material that is sung in Mass today, much of it is rather trite and "fluffy". Let's face it: moody male teenagers who are staying away from Mass today are unlikely to return to sing songs about love and peace. The last word to Mary Kenny in the *Irish Catholic*:

"The danger in making any institution more 'feminised' is that you alienate young men, who need to affirm their masculinity, and for whom any form of 'petticoat rule' is anathema. This is in the hard wiring of their brains: they can't help it . . . as it increasingly becomes a 'woman's profession', men recoil from it."

#12

Promote and sell spiritual books and magazines for young people at Mass

Sister Malachy O'Farrell suggests *Power for Living* magazine for young people. Other excellent publications such as *Face Up* and *Alive* are also readily available in most Churches. However, I have seldom — if ever — heard a priest specifically refer to these during Mass. With film and music reviews as well as topical youth issues contained within their pages, there's plenty of scope for a little "plug" during a sermon, which might at least raise awareness of their existence.

#13

The Church is a community — build the Church's community spirit

There are obviously many ways for this to be done; later ideas such as "Stations" and greater interaction at Mass are probably part of the solution. People have also called on priests to be more "visible" in their communities:

"They could work in paid employment," Judy O'Brien says, "marry or not as they so choose, join local clubs . . . i.e. do what 'real people do'."

#14

Have women priests

The debate concerning whether — as Kerryman Donal Sugrue put it — having "birds as priests" would attract more churchgoers will rage on, apparently. Yet it is interesting to note that Mr Sugrue was one of the few contributors to refer to what one might believe from media coverage is a hotly contested subject.

#15

Have married priests

Despite its perception as another of the Church's "hot potatoes" in the media and society, the married priests issue was only mentioned by six per cent of respondents. Tellingly, all but one of the six per cent was young.

Debbie Brennan's argument is that married priests "will have the experience and proper knowledge when giving advice about marriage, relationships, etc." Is this valid? Does one, for example, need to have been pregnant to counsel a pregnant woman? My training and work with Cura tells me otherwise. In this regard, another contributor asks, "How can a priest preach about something that he cannot understand?" The implication is that one cannot give advice or even speak about something unless one has experienced it. Yet, this clearly does not apply to drugs, crime or more pertinently, marriage counselling. Still, this attitude is certainly "out there", so it probably needs to be addressed.

Seamus Allard's viewpoint was a little different; he himself considered the priesthood. "The only drawback was, of course, no girls," he says. Would the introduction of married priests bring more people like Seamus flocking to the priesthood? Maybe so, but I'll leave the last word to 90 priests from the Arlington Diocese of Illinois. In a letter to their Bishop, the priests rejected a proposal by Milwaukee priests in 2003 that called for the ordination of married men to generate more vocations to the priesthood.

"Common sense and historical experience," they said, "indicate that reducing the demands of the priesthood will not increase vocations, because lessening sacrifice never inspires men to offer their lives to Christ."

#16

Set up a dating agency for young Catholics

My research for this book partly took me to the Bankers Club by St Stephen's Green to see what Hugh Hanley's "Thirtysomethings" was all about (see Appendix). One inevitable side-effect when one places like-minded (mostly) single males and females of that age in the same room is that dating or attempted dating will follow. My wife and I both went in anticipation of a spiritual dimension (which did belatedly arrive in the form of a beautiful Advent ceremony, attended by five other people), but both agreed that for many in the group, the spiritual aspect was somewhat secondary to social and relationship opportunities. From my experiences of the "Thirtysomethings", I certainly believe that, in this age of speed-dating, an opportunity exists for the Church to provide a similar, but wider social network for young, unattached people to form friendships and possible relationships in a subtle religious context. Indeed, look no further than UK website "Christian Connection", which has proved so successful that its founder, Jackie Elton, is bringing it to Ireland, along with Christian speed-dating. While the site www.christianconnection.ie appears aimed at Christians of all types, it certainly paves the way for a Catholic version.

#17

Tone down Church condemnation of gays

"Do not lie with a man as one lies with a woman; it is an abomination." — *Leviticus 19:22*

In a commencement address this year at Georgetown University, Papal candidate Cardinal Arinze drew protests by saying the institution of marriage is "mocked by homosexuality". One can only imagine the reaction of gay Catholics to such a statement. One such reaction was submitted for this book:

"How can I feel anything but indifference bordering on antipathy for an institution such as the Catholic Church?" the person writes. The Church is described as "mired in medieval bigotry" and guilty of "mesmerising hypocrisy". Such strong feelings are unlikely to wane with the use of rhetoric like "evil", "immoral" and "dangerous", and while the relevant Biblical text in *Leviticus* is clear and unambiguous, so is the hurt caused by condemnatory tones. Could language used be more diplomatic, to negate another contributor's strongly held perception that "if you are gay, the Church will not accept you?"

#18

Encourage youth to do voluntary work

With lack of time frequently cited as a reason not to do voluntary work by adults, perhaps young adults, without the opportunity cost of full-time paid work, might emerge as the volunteers of the future. Incorporating such an experience in a transition year or Leaving Certificate course might be a path worth taking. Alternatively, Michael McCullagh's finding that young people "benefit enormously from 'mission' abroad" could be explored via aid agencies and missionary organisations. "Young people are", as Patsy McGarry points out, "generally, idealistic. They are also compassionate. And they like to 'do' — to be active." And Sister Stan says: "Young

people like to be challenged. . . . Young people are idealistic — they need to express themselves through freedom
and authenticity. Young people have huge energy and
they need to express it in love of self and love of
neighbour." In terms of voluntary work, the ingredients
are all there.

#19

Be a strong voice and campaign
on social issues

Few people "do" social issues like Peter McVerry, and his
assertion that "unless the Church is struggling to bring
justice to those on the margins of our national societies
and our global society, then its preaching that we are all
children of God is a sham" strikes to the core of this thesis. "Hence, I believe," he adds, "that the Church ought
to be on the side of those on the margins, supporting
their struggle for a rightful place in our society and a fair
share of the resources of our planet, being their voice
and helping them to articulate their own just demands."

Mountjoy Governor John Lonergan echoes this in
urging the Church to "become much more vocal and active around social and justice issues".

#20

Give positive advice and support around the suicide issue

"Out of the depths I cry to you,
O Lord hear my voice!"
Psalm 130.1

According to Mary Hanafin, "one of the more alarming indicators of young people's difficulty in accepting and adapting to social change is the phenomenal increase in the incidences of suicide among young men in the past 15 years. There has been a 79 per cent increase in the number of young men committing suicide in Ireland since 1989." Why is this? Marie Taylor remarks that "people carry around so many worries and pain; I think the Church should be helping people to help themselves". Services such as the suicide counselling provided by the Blessed Sacrament Chapel on Bachelor's Quay (Tel 01-8724597) are a start — but the need is clearly there for more of the same.

#21

Campaign to get families to pray together

"The Family that prays together stays together" has become one of Catholicism's most familiar quotes, and some contributors couldn't resist reiterating its logic. Yet, how many families do pray together? And how many young people will join in? If, as Nora Bennis reminds us, "the future of the world passes by way of the family", is the family home, and not the Church, the ideal starting point for greater faith?

#22

Have adults as good examples and witnesses of their faith

In his letters to the Corinthians, Paul called us to be "ambassadors for Christ". While bearing witness may not be the traditional Irish way of practising Catholicism, "evangelisation lies at the heart of the mission of the Church", as Dr Diarmuid Martin is now reminding us. Indeed, the new Archbishop has made evangelisation his primary focus. Just as Jesus urged us to let our lights shine before others, Brendan Tarrant says, "when young people see our faith in action, they will be encouraged to follow". And Bishop Willie Walsh reiterates this by saying, "young people will not be impressed by what we say or preach; they will be influenced by the way they see us living our lives".

#23

Educate people about the Rosary and distribute free beads

Though the Pope recently added five new "Mysteries of Light" to the 15 decades of the Rosary, it hasn't exactly stirred young people in their droves to clutch their beads and start novenas. Still, a number of people suggested the Rosary as the answer to this book's central question. Sean O'Farrell considered it "imperative to have a strong prayer life in the family home — particularly the Rosary". Another, Kathleen Quinn, has actively pursued this, praying the Rosary with six young children, while her namesake Kathleen Hally advises that "each child should be requested to have plastic Rosary beads."

Perhaps with some specific education as to the Rosary's origin, purpose and benefits, young people might start to take up their beads and pray with them again.

#24

Explain the Church's purpose and structure

The hierarchical structure of the Catholic Church has been under attack for centuries. This is no different today, where, for some, the Church's layers of authority serve as a popular and convenient beating stick. "As an institution," Cardinal Connell writes, "the Church is exposed to current anti-institutional resentment. Yet essential to the Church is the institutional structure that enables it to endure the passage of time and to serve the unity of its membership." Conveying this message to a cynical audience is a different matter, of course. Yet what big multinational corporation could operate efficiently in modern times without a hierarchical structure, one wonders? The Church, for Matthew, is the "ante-chamber" of the kingdom of God, according to A.N. Wilson (1998); but in

modern times, it is also aided by PR consultants and marketing experts. Perhaps a simple explanation — historical
and operational — concerning the need for Cardinals,
Archbishops, Bishops and the Pope wouldn't go amiss?

#25

Promote the good work of the Church more loudly

Like any large institution, the Church benefits from good
PR from time to time. Former Fine Gael leader John
Bruton provided a good example recently, when speaking to UCD students. "The Church," he said, provides a
means whereby believers can find eternal salvation. Provides a window through which people can glimpse the
possibility of life after death . . . that is where the
Church's real success is to be found." Mr Bruton referred
to education and health services provided by the Church
and thanked it for "preaching a message that is funda-
mentally true" and standing up for the right to life,
where "utilitarian and non-believers might have cast
such human life aside".

The Church's appeal is undeniably correlated with its
reputation; while negative stories have received remarkable amounts of media space, there is a flip-side — as the
high-profile case of exonerated nun, Nora Wall, illus-
trates. Whether it's Nora's testimony (which she kindly
submitted to me during my research on this book) or a
politician's, the good work of the Church and the injus-
tices it has suffered deserve a better airing.

Speaking about child abuse, Michael Egan says, "all those virtuous priests, the vast majority of whom wouldn't think of committing such crimes, should be remembered". Development worker Terence Fitzgerald speaks of his "very positive views of missionaries . . . in Sierra Leone and Kenya devoting their lives to the poor"; another contributor admits that the "Church did have a lot to do in shaping the person I am today" and adds that "the Church helps members of society that everyone else ignores", recognising the "genuine devotion of some priests and nuns to God". What these last three contributors have in common is that they are (a) quite critical of the Church initially and (b) quite young.

Behind even its harshest critics is an awareness and acknowledgement of the Church's contribution to Irish society. There is no harm in reminding people modestly about society's debt to the Church and the invisible Church whose good deeds are seldom acknowledged.

#26

Quit talking about the Church and talk more about God and the Bible

While most people just answered my question, some people answered by challenging the question itself. Born-again Christian John D. Nugent thought it should be re-phrased to focus on God rather than the Church. "Who," he asks, amongst young people, "wants to strengthen their commitment to the Church of all things?" Pointing out that "most of them have time for God", he suggests that commitment to God should be the first stepping-stone with youth, and perhaps he has a point.

#27

Campaign to clarify Sunday as a special day for God

You don't have to be old to remember the days when almost every shop was closed on a Sunday. In the last decade, all that has changed — and changed utterly. So why is it that, in the words of Rebecca Leavy, "lots of people would consider themselves to be religious people, but choose not to go to Mass?" Is this the allure of the shopping mall or an indictment of Mass itself? And why has a centuries-honoured Commandment suddenly been cast aside? If Mass time has been reduced to what Janet O'Connor refers to as "first thing Sunday morning when we're sleeping off our hangovers", then it's surely time for a campaign to get Sunday back on the map.

#28

Use humour more

For centuries, the Easter liturgy contained laughter as an intrinsic component. "Easter laughter" (*ritual paschalis*) as it was known was purposefully provoked by preachers in German-speaking countries, sometimes to the point of violent bursts of laughter.

If half the ads on TV use humour, then why not priests? They are, after all, walking/talking advertisements for their faith, and, for the "floating voters" among the congregation a humorous priest can keep them coming back. Lorraine Keane speaks of driving for an hour to attend a Mass, which she leaves with a smile on her face. Speaking of speeches, almost all best-man speeches — even the nervous ones — combine humour and sincerity effectively. How different is a sermon to a best-man speech, except Jesus is the groom to be praised?

#29

Issue clear teaching on new sins, e.g. false claims and ticket touting

An observation that did the rounds once was that the Eleventh Commandment in Ireland is "Thou shalt not get caught". A variation of this theme is that when an activity isn't specifically referred to in Scripture, it can't be sinful. In Ireland today, we are plagued by new types of "sin", which have thus far avoided heavy condemnation. False claims — be they insurance or abuse-related — are clearly hurtful and wrong. Along with perjury — another topical issue in today's legal process — they are covered by the Eighth Commandment ("Thou shalt not bear false witness . . ."), just as ticket touting is cornered by the Seventh ("Thou shalt not steal"). By constantly providing guidance and clarification as such issues arise in society, the Church might at least show itself as being in touch with modern issues.

Conversely, what Gillian O'Sullivan puts forward is still pertinent and worthy of emphasis: "the focus point

should be that the moral values of goodness, honesty
and kindness are still relevant and important in modern-
day situations."

#30

End the money racket at First
Communions, Confirmations
and Christmas

"So Jesus went to the Temple and drove out all who were
buying and selling in the temple area. He overturned the
tables of the moneychangers, and the stools of those who
sold pigeons. And he said to them, 'It is written: My
house will be called a house of prayer. But you have
turned it into a den of thieves'. *Matthew 21: 12-13*

Every Christmas, Christians lament its decline into
materialism. Each year, also, children's Holy Communion and Confirmation days are frequently cited as inap-
propriately lavish occasions, with far too much money
involved. This has become a topical issue in 2004, addressed by some high-profile religious figures. That
Christmas, Communions and Confirmations have become synonymous with money and material gifts is not
ideal; the fact that they are also synonymous with im-
pressionable children is more worrying and pertinent.

#31

Elect a young non-European Pope (and engage young people in the process)

Despite the seismic impact of the Pope's visit in 1979, a contributor born in that very year refers to him as "an ageing role model with little or no relevance to young people". While wagers such as Paddy Power's on the identity of the next Pope have been condemned as neither "acceptable nor moral" by Church authorities, those of us present in 1979 can vouch for the impetus of a young, non-Italian Pope, with a sense of humour. As Mary Kenny writes, "there is nothing distasteful about making preparations for events after our deaths . . . so why should it be wrong to speculate on what might happen after the death of some very great person?" She adds that "the Papal betting game is positively good publicity. It creates huge interest in the Catholic Church as a universal power."

As we have seen with *You're a Star*, *Big Brother* and *Celebrity Farm*, young people love a contest. Engaging young people about the possible candidates may at least enliven their interest in the next leader of their Church. Can that be a bad thing?

#32

Have a Vatican III to shake and freshen up the Church

The Second Vatican Council's principal aim was to promote renewal of the life of the Church, yet while Vatican II's influence on the Church and Catholicism has been phenomenal, would it be timely to have a "clean-the-air" Vatican III without the weighty theological documents and controversial statements? Such an event might set simple, but strict new precedents for child abuse and focus on making the Church more attractive for its future generations.

#33

Sunday school for children instead of Mass

"Jesus then said, 'Let them be! Do not stop the children from coming to me, for the kingdom of Heaven belongs to people such as these.'" — *Matthew 19:13*

A letter to the *Irish Catholic* (6 November 2003) defending Father Martin Tierney pointed out that he has "appointed a full-time youth pastor who runs a children's ministry on a Wednesday evening and a Gospel time for children during the 12 o'clock Mass". The concept of segregating adults and children for the mutual benefit of their religious formation is not a new one, but it seems to require entrepreneurial efforts like Fr Martin's to make it part and parcel of the Catholic system here.

Ironically, Ruth O'Sullivan, who suggests "Church mother and toddler groups" and "Sunday schools", grew up with Methodist and Baptist attendance and was raised in a Protestant family. I have frequently observed how relatively well versed in scripture young people of other Christian churches are compared to their Catholic counterparts on this island. For the reasons above, there is a definite argument, as Noreen McKeone promotes, "that Sunday school would help kids to become familiar with the Bible and give them a good moral understanding".

#34

Set up Church groups especially for teenagers

Not all teenagers are as brave as contributor Aaron Mullaney, who has set up his own spiritual group, "Teen Spirit". However, the same need which inspired Aaron undoubtedly exists in teenagers in every parish. By meeting this need directly, the Church may keep more of its lambs in the fold.

#35

Set up groups where young Christians can socialise together

Hugh Hanley's "Twentysomethings" and "Thirtysomethings" (see Appendix) are great examples of how young Catholics can meet socially. There is also an apostolate that has had some successful pilot programmes in Dublin called "Theology on Tap" (age 20+). The latter involves "a pub of good repute, one speaker on topics of general spiritual interest, questions and answers and a pint". According to Fr Martin O'Connor at the Dal Riada centre in Blackrock, the feedback has been excellent. Other groups such as Youth 2000 are featured in Appendix A.

#36

Weekend youth retreats based on spirituality and also fun

Retreat Director Sister Una Kearney believes that retreats offer an ideal opportunity for young people to "encounter a witness who is living the Gospel with joy within the Church community". If this is, as Sister Una claims, "the greatest incentive to commitment for a young person", perhaps retreats are the answer!

#37

Challenge the hollow cult of celebrity and show the contrasting substance of religion

That we live in an age of celebrity culture is beyond debate, but many will also agree that its protagonists are far from ideal role models and that the culture itself lacks substance or meaning. "There is clearly a vacuum in Irish society," Mary Hanafin maintains, "and the challenge facing us now is what we choose to fill that vacuum. The Church and the Christian message it brings have something valuable and timely to offer in this respect."

#38

Re-package the Church as a club that young people are an important part of

In this era of fitness clubs, supermarket club cards and supporters' clubs, people are constantly being asked to join clubs. Members of such clubs are encouraged to use their membership actively when they do join. Can the Catholic Church afford to act differently, by assuming a Confirmed child is a confirmed life member?

Bishop John Buckley of Cork and Ross certainly doesn't think so: "Commitment must be nurtured, nourished, supported and strengthened at local level. Parishes that have invited young people to become involved at a liturgical and parish council level have been enriched by the contributions made and . . . young people and their faith commitment have benefited too. . . . The contribution of young people must always be encouraged and sought. That is a challenge for all involved in Church."

#39

Redefine religion as being more than just Mass on Sunday

Given expressed opinions about Mass being boring for young people, e.g. "I do not attend church. I find it quite boring and a waste of time", it is surely crucial to convey the message that Catholicism is indeed far more than just Mass. If Sunday Mass is understood to be the "be all and end all" of Catholicism, what hope is there for those who find it "quite boring and a waste of time"?

#40

A Catholic radio station that focuses on topical youth issues and plays good music

Such a station, 89.9 Spirit FM, has just won a short-term licence to broadcast at weekends and won favourable reviews following initial broadcasts. The success of such a venture requires publicity via the Churches, but there is undoubtedly a plethora of stations in Dublin playing the same music, so a niche definitely exists. There is enough "cool" Christian music out there to play, and the station has pledged to contain 80 per cent "contemporary Christian" in its mix. As we all know, a portion of Christian music can be decidedly "dodgy", especially to the discerning young listener; but for every "dodgy" Christian song, there's "Way Down in the Hole" by Tom Waits, U2's "Walk On", The Neville Brothers' "Will the Circle Be Unbroken", Bob Dylan's "Gotta Serve Somebody" and Low's "Lordy".

#41

Recommend good/suitable films/music/TV at weekend Masses

The *Irish Catholic* contains a section each week previewing the week ahead on television and radio — it also previews books and movies. Something similar during Mass or in the parish newsletter might wake a few teenagers up!

#42

Advertise where young people have thinking time, e.g. DART stations, toilet doors, etc.

Contributor Paula Walsh's bus journey on the Stillorgan dual carriageway may not cause her to think of God, but a simple advertising venture by a local church does. "The little church always has slogans," she remarks; "at the moment, 'church' is written 'ch...ch', then underneath 'where R U?'" Like all commercial advertising these days, one must fight for the attention of one's target audience where they are at and where they have time to absorb the message you wish to convey. Whether that's on a bus route, train platform, toilet door, till receipt, cinema ticket or a plain old "BCI-approved" 30-second commercial during *Coronation Street*, it can still pay to advertise.

#43

Invite young people to be more involved, e.g. readings, parish newsletter

Involvement and participation were two of the most common themes in Part 1. Fr Colm Kilcoyne suspects that "any worthwhile answer has to do with involvement/work they can get their teeth into". Participation, according to Mary Coughlan, nurtures interest in young people. "By being involved, by participating," she states, "people will find themselves drawn to the Church —

whether it's through more discussion on the future of the Church or through more contact with representatives of the Church."

"What," she and many others might ask, "has the Church done recently that made young people want to get involved, to identify with their Church?"

Unless one gives them "space and responsibility", as Agnes Haverty advocates, they may see little or no reason to participate. In this context, Fr John Wall maintains (with 30 years experience) that "any group that provides accompaniment to young people, in the context of basic Gospel values, will . . . allow the Spirit to take root and a young church to flower".

#44

Use interesting people from the community and good speakers for sermons

We frequently encounter missionaries and charity representatives speaking after the Gospel about their experiences and requesting donations. While some of these "life stories" are captivating, much of the material probably *feels* of little or no relevance to younger people in attendance. However, there is a case to be made, as Louisa Glennon does, for "educated lay people (trained in catechetics and communications) giving the odd sermon".

#45

Each parish should have special Masses and groups just for young people

Special youth Masses usually mean "Folk Masses", and as Lorcan Ó hAlmhain contends, this can ironically be a turn-off for young people. Does a Mass necessarily need to have a folk or musical element to be a "youth Mass"? The mutual support of being in the company of like-minded young people is possibly the actual dynamic that galvanises the faith of many young people. It is this sense of belonging that is touched upon by many contributors, especially those involved in groups. Simply making such Masses and groups available within a parish could be enough to make a difference.

#46

Explain Vatican wealth and sell some to give to the poor

A complaint from some people who visit the Vatican concerns its opulence. This sometimes leads to statements concerning poverty and suggestions that the former might be used to alleviate the latter. If this is not a valid course of action, perhaps those who propose it ought to be informed as to why.

#47

A consistent and zero tolerance policy on proven child abuse from now on

What hasn't been said on the topic of clerical child abuse? Young contributor Michael Egan expresses the attitude of many when he says: "The anguish and suffering which those people had to and continue to endure should not be ignored — which may have been the case in years gone by. The acts committed should be accountable to civil law and not hidden behind Canon Law . . . [the] failure to be upfront is part of the reason why the media continues to have their field days and damage the credibility of the Church in this country."

Columnist and commentator Ronan Mullen sees a broader problem with all this: "while the exposure of scandals has helped to make people more accountable," he says, "the corresponding loss of trust in people and institutions is bad news. We are made more cynical about life when other people's failures get disproportionate attention. Where good news is no news, our willingness to learn from each other's wisdom and life experience is lessened."

#48

Better training for priests more suitable to the modern world

While studies such as that conducted recently in Bishop Willie Walsh's diocese appear to affirm the high regard in which most lay people hold clergy, a strong collective voice appears to be calling for better training for priests in some areas. As Sean O'Farrell laments, "the young priests don't seem to be trained on pastoral or evangelisation. Our mature clergy," he continues, "must regularly undergo refresher courses on how to sell themselves and put the message in a modern way — to meet modern demands and needs and to make it relevant."

#49

Younger priests who are approachable to work with young people

While the high average age of priests and religious is a phenomenon of vocations trends over the last 60 or 70 years, it is undeniably a turn-off to many young people. "Take away the old people who want to control everything", one young person says! Conversely, Michael Egan notes that "when there is a relatively young (25–55 years) and active priest in the parish, the youth become more involved and willing to participate in activities both within and outside of the Church".

#50

Redefine prayer in terms of feeding poor, visiting sick, etc.

While not all young people pray in a traditional sense, they are, as Patsy McGarry maintains, "idealistic . . . they are also compassionate . . . and they like to 'do'." In emphasising the virtue of charity through active "doing" the Church may attract some young people who are not drawn to conventional prayer. Fr Jim Stanley says: "My one suggestion is: 'invite and engage them in any worthwhile project that involves service and giving' — not just talking, discussion thinking and praying, important as all these are. When we begin to serve and to do, things happen. God responds and in the giving, we receive and the kingdom of God begins to grow."

#51

Have young committed Christians bearing witness to their faith

Martin Tierney's contribution says, "to strengthen commitment within the Church, I would encourage young people already committed to Christ to witness to their faith without fear". As if to illustrate this point, fellow religious Eilis Bergin speaks of "two teenage schoolboys who had returned from a visit to Calcutta in India, where they had spent some time helping the poor. This experience had brought their faith to life and had a great influence on their classmates."

Bishop Leo O'Reilly reminds us, "you never really learn a subject until you have taught it. The same applies here. Get young people involved in ministry. Empower them to bring the message of Jesus to others of the same age or younger. In doing that, they will appreciate that message in an altogether new way. It will deepen their own conviction and their commitment as well as sharing their own faith with others."

#52

Encourage people to wear blessed symbols of faith, e.g. cross, ring, scapular etc.

Cliona Ní Ghiolla laments the fact that "children are bored at Mass and haven't children's books, holy pictures and medals". The latter part of her argument could be debated — many young people wear symbols of their faith — but, unfortunately, this is an age where a crucifix can be considered either "sexy" (Madonna) or merely fashionable. The wearing of religious symbols — like many other acts today — obviously has merit, but its meaning has to be accentuated.

#53

Present Jesus as a friend who's always there for you and worth getting to know

Cardinal Connell's piece says the following, and it sums up this thesis: "At the heart of Christian faith there is a mystical call addressed to us all and not just to the saints. It has to do with 'the knowledge of Christ'. This is not knowledge about Christ such as scholars may acquire through research, whether or not they have faith. It resembles much more the personal knowledge that grows out of our human experience of friendship. As St Augustine says: 'One comes to know a person only through friendship'." (*De Div Quaest. LXXI:5*).

One young man who has encountered such a friendship is "Teen Spirit's" Aaron Mullaney, who was unsuccessfully trying to avoid a retreat when he found God instead: "The beauty of having Jesus in your life," he proclaims, "is that He has you and you have Him. There is no stronger bond than that and nothing or nobody can break it. Unfortunately, young people like myself are not given the opportunity of making the best friend they'll ever have."

#54

Acknowledge the Devil's existence and the need to combat evil by doing good deeds

The days of preaching fire and brimstone are gone and some might argue that belief in the Devil has gone with them. George Lynch says that "while conducting a 'Growing in Faith' programme with post-confirmation teenagers none believed that the Devil exists or that evil is a reality in the world". One need only assess the contrasting impact of the release of *The Exorcist* in 1973 and its re-release in 1998 to see how attitudes to and fear of the Devil has changed. Joseph Foyle of the "Foil the Devil" crusade argues that "few now do things to foil the devil. Most people," he says, "do not even think about him. Their preachers do not remind them enough." Is, as Joseph believes, belief in the Devil part of the secret in reviving belief in "doing good"?

#55

Teach young people a short daily and weekly prayer routine

As Bill Gallagher from Donegal says, "God gave you 168 hours a week — why not give Him just a half-hour . . . just go for that short time every week. He will do the rest."

#56

Ensure young people know the basics and can explain what their faith is all about

Improving knowledge of the basics of the faith was the second biggest challenge facing the Church according to contributors, so I will merely quote two of those who expressed this opinion:

"Solid doctrine needs to be taught today . . . if we get that right, we can build our faith" — Sr Josepha O'Donnell.

"My answer is that they must be able to understand and explain their faith" — Sr Bríd Ní Rinn.

#57

Speak the language of young people, e.g. films, football, music, relationships

If the chart-topping band Evanescence were to be mentioned in a sermon, few in attendance would have any idea who they were, but a large proportion of young people would. So what, I hear you say; many chart-topping acts come and go without making any impression on people over the age of 30. Yet Evanescence are not just a chart-topping band, they are a Christian rock band. So it is somewhat surprising that a Church that is struggling for links with today's youth has not embraced their huge success. In the same breath, one might mention Dashboard Confessional and Low — other Christian artists not afraid to discuss their faith, who — unlike Daniel O'Donnell and Cliff Richard — are in possession of "street cred". Closer to home, Bono and leading English bands Coldplay and Radiohead are all actively committed to causes like the Samaritans, Oxfam and the elimination of Third World debt. Obviously, being a Christian or a do-gooder has not gone out of fashion.

Speaking the language of youth doesn't necessarily mean "getting down" with the MTV generation, but some basic education of this type would definitely help to forge links with a disenchanted generation. As Marc Sheridan says, "If you get it right, you become accepted . . . but not for long, as you need to change with their needs to remain relevant/credible." Marc puts words to the attitude of many young people when he says, "if you're not willing to meet my needs, my trends (respect me) then why should I bother with you?" Thus, speaking their language — or at least being seen to try to understand it — is probably a good idea.

#58

Promote Fair Trade products and educate concerning globalisation

In a consumption-driven society, sometimes the best one can hope for is that people will make ethical decisions when purchasing! Globalisation and Fair Trade have reared their heads significantly over the last decade, yet I've never heard a sermon addressing these topics. If Fair Trade products tackle poverty and injustice in the developing world, they are surely worthy of promotion. Conversely, if products are being produced in conditions that involve unfair working conditions, they too are worthy of mention.

#59

Run a Church campaign to encourage charitable use of mature SSIAs

In 2007, the biggest windfall in Irish history takes place, when billions of euro are released from mature SSIA accounts. This temporary release of enormous funds presents a unique opportunity for the Church to be innovative and constructive in helping people to consider noble causes.

#60

Campaign for and encourage a non-judgemental reaction to teenage pregnancy

"Do not judge and you will not be judged. In the same way you judge others, you will be judged, and the measure you use for others will be used for you." *Matthew 7:1-2.*

As a pregnancy counsellor in my past, I have long contended that fear of parental reaction has led to more abortions than most other contributory factors. The irony is, of course, that the worst offenders when it comes to parental fear are often staunchly anti-abortion parents. Thus, it is little wonder that young people can equate deeply held religious views with intolerance. As John Costello puts it, "I have been put off by priests mouthing off about unmarried mothers". Educating priests and parents as to the negative impact of such an approach might just win over some "put-off" teenagers and save a few unborn lives.

#61

Have house blessings by a local priest or a special "house blessing" minister

In an age where suburban dwellers are quite likely to be strangers to both their neighbours and parish priest, house blessings may be more relevant than ever. For young people, even the symbolism of such a gesture or ceremony can have a strong impact. For Mary Kenny, "such traditions as blessing the home . . . are very, very relevant".

#62

Instruct parents at baptism about their faith and about bringing children up in the faith

For some, the problems of faith not being passed on properly begin at baptism. Gertie McEnroe believes that "parents and godparents should have instruction on their duties; if they're not practising, there's little chance for the child".

#63

Re-introduce "Stations of the Cross" in homes and help neighbourhood spirit

One of the social events of the rural community was, and possibly still is in some areas, the Stations of the Cross. Louisa Glennon recommends its revival, emphasising its social aspect and suggesting "the local coffee shop" as an alternative location. If a "new-look Stations" were to incorporate such ideas, then statements such as Mary Kenny's that "the Stations of the Cross are beautiful and enriching and provide the inner life of the faith" might be uttered by young people too.

#64

Have Confirmation at the age of 16 or 17 when people can make better choices

"Take the Sacrament of Confirmation out of the primary schools — and, indeed, out of the school altogether. Let the Sacrament be given around 16 years of age, and organised through the parishes. In order to qualify for the Sacrament, the young people would have to do a course of preparation in the local parish over a period to be set down. Perhaps a common national date could be designated (e.g. Pentecost Sunday) as the suitable date for Confirmation Sunday. Details might differ in different circumstances, but of the general idea, I am very deeply convinced." — Fr Con Breen.

#65

Adapt modern songs that young people like for use in Mass as long as they have a Christian message

"Sing to the Lord a new song." *Psalm 96.*

Cáit Breathnach makes the point (well) that "young people are moved, often passionately, by music. Music performers have become their heroes". It may be a bridge too far to play Eminem at Mass, as John Costello suggests, but lyrics from modern songs — such as "Lord Can You Hear Me?" by Low and "Down to the River to Pray" by Alison Krauss, or the refrain from Leonard Cohen/Jeff Buckley's "Hallelujah" — could easily be moulded into tremendously effective Taize chants. This may require a little creativity and imagination but it's crucial (as Seamus Ahearne points out) that for young people we don't become "a museum for visiting or observing . . . but rather an energetic, imaginative and youthful community full of artistic excitement where the young are really at home and find space for their enthusiasm and ideals".

#66

Present idea that you can be a dedicated Christian and "cool" and point out well-known young people who are both

Janet O'Connor contends that, "a lot of young people feel that the most un-cool thing they could do is to go to church on a Sunday". It begs the question: if "cool"

Christian people, who go to Mass, were pointed out to them, would they change their stance?

#67

Set up a Third World child sponsorship campaign from primary school onwards for Irish children

Despite role models like Bono and Bob Geldof, Irish children have grown up in an environment of increasing prosperity since the 1980s, largely oblivious to their privileged status compared to their counterparts in the developing world. While child sponsorship is a popular form of charitable donation among adults (both World Vision and the Christian Children's Fund have thriving Irish branches), the benefits of child-to-child contact via sponsorship and letters could be developed. Whether funding comes from parents, the State, the Church or a mixture of these, a Third World-sponsored child for every Irish school child would be a wonderful vision. The Church could be instrumental in setting up such a project.

#68

Encourage people to bless themselves or pray in daily moments — be it passing graveyards or exams

Most Irish people recall Packie Bonner's penalty save in the 1990 World Cup. Some of us might also recall that Packie blessed himself prior to that save. Modern hero Damien Duff has a habit of blessing himself before playing. The act, though simple, is a powerful reminder that God is ever ready for contact; this fact could benefit from being reinforced. Whether it's before an exam or a match, when a bell tolls, or while an ambulance or fire engine passes, every day has many moments when such contact can be made. It may be still thought of by some as what Mary Kenny calls "old-fashioned devotion", but the Sign of the Cross need not be.

#69

Set up a specially approved text number for God — people could text their "prayers" to this number as a form of prayer

The preferred language of youth today is undeniably "phone-text"! If we are hoping to speak the language of youth, it might be wise to look into the way they communicate. The recently introduced "thought for the day" text from the Pope may have surprised some (see Appendix C). So what about a text in the other direction?

Young people may not wish to visit a church to pray but might be persuaded to "text" a prayer to a given number. If you can deliver a prayer to "God's post-box" in the Wailing Wall, why not have a Vatican-approved "God's Inbox" if youth feel comfortable communicating with Him in that way?

#70

Focus on good day-to-day deeds — and less on going to Mass — as a way of being a good Catholic

"I was hungry and you fed me, I was thirsty and you gave me drink. I was a stranger and you welcomed me into your house. I was naked and you clothed me. I was sick and you visited me. I was in prison and you went to see me." — *Matthew 25:34*

With so many young people expressing misgivings about Mass, it is clearly beneficial to present Catholicism as being about more than Mass attendance — something that is backed strongly by New Testament texts.

#71

Draw up a charter for Christian behaviour in schools/workplace regarding honesty, homework, texts, e-mails, gossip etc.

The recent case of a pornographic image of a schoolgirl being circulated by camera phone across the country highlights the need for ethics in every aspect of our day-to-day lives, and the consequences of a completely liberal ethos. The Church's voice and guidance on such matters, even if it's only for parents, can provide for a safer society. Moses' flock needed boundaries and guidelines and today's society is no different.

#72

Promote alternatives to materialism and provide best policy regarding Lotto wins, SSIAs, etc. based on Gospel teachings

John Lennon's "Imagine" springs to mind when reading Michael Breen's eloquent contribution. Among his list of seven "Imagines" was a Lennon-esque aspiration: "Imagine what the Church might be like where people were given priority over possessions." *Irish Times* columnist, Breda O'Brien agrees: "We need to model an alternative to the sometimes mindless consumerism which is being peddled today."

Indeed, surely a Church based on a man who spoke of rich men and heaven in terms of camels and eyes of needles should offer such a model, and rally against materialism?

#73

Ask young people at what times they would like to have Mass and arrange special youth Mass times

In her study of this same topic, advertising diploma graduate Louisa Glennon calls on the Church to "make Mass times more accessible in order to entice youth attendance — maybe at intervals from 4.00 pm to 8.00 pm on Sundays".

#74

Bring back the traditional sense of awe and mystery around Mass — incense, Gregorian chants etc. in stylish ceremony

A small number of contributors mention the Latin Mass and other traditional practices wistfully. "Fr William" of Mellifont Abbey runs a Traditional Mass and wrote to mention positive feedback such as "we love the Latin Mass, Father, for we feel you are praying more for us when you also face the cross and tabernacle". Mary Kenny remarks that "really old-fashioned devotion, the more spiritual, the better, is absolutely vital". When one considers that Mel Gibson's widely screened new movie, *The Passion of the Christ,* is in Latin and Aramaic, perhaps the Latin Mass isn't necessarily ready for the scrap heap! The revival of Gregorian chant via the multimillion selling dance music act Enigma could hardly have been predicted — but was proof positive that a traditional sense of mystery and awe can be attractive to younger generations. The exhilarating chants of monks in Enigma's "Sadness Part 1" and "Mea Culpa", and the religious singing on *The Mission* soundtrack have attracted young people in their millions — so why not the real thing too?

#75

Have a Great Sign of Peace once a month or so, where everyone shakes hands with each other

One part of Mass that gets most people smiling is the Sign of Peace. Do we overlook its mobilising power? Aside from being a potential healer of rifts and its feel-good factor, the Sign of Peace is wonderfully symbolic and simple, and sometimes it just seems too short. In an age where congregations are often complete strangers to each other, an occasional "Great Sign of Peace" — possibly at the end of the Mass — where people shake hands for an extended period, could be an ideal ice-breaker and a force to generate community spirit.

#76

Make Catholicism a Leaving Cert subject that students might find interesting and useful for getting high points

While Religious Education has become a proper school subject again, the syllabus has not been universally acclaimed, and the retention of facts is far from the days of the Penny Catechism. The deeply held view of many contributors that the Catholic faith is not being passed on in the school system is unlikely to change until Catholicism — rather than religion — is offered as an examinable subject instead of a vague "doss class", as is sometimes the case. As Louisa Glennon remarks, "if taught properly it could be very interesting and increase people's knowledge of scripture and theology". It might at least ensure that those who choose to study it would take it seriously.

#77

Leaving Cert module: study movies with religious themes like *Jesus of Montreal*, *Se7en*, and *The Exorcist*

Writing in the *Irish Catholic*, the topic of religious movies was covered quite comprehensively by Aubrey Malone (6 November 2003). "Perhaps the most moving of all was presented to us in 1966," he writes, "in *The Gospel According to St Matthew* . . . by a Marxist atheist, Paolo Pasolini". Indeed, this version has been widely acclaimed as Christ's finest hour on celluloid. Unlike expriesthood-student Martin Scorsese's challenging, earnest, but controversial *Last Temptation of Christ* or Denys Arcand's exceedingly clever *Jesus of Montreal*, Pasolini's movie has a 15 Certificate, and is thus apt for study by Leaving Certificate students. Other flawed, but English-language attempts exist, of course, with Robert Powell and Max Von Sydow's roles in *Jesus of Nazareth* and *The Greatest Story Ever Told* among the best. With Mel Gibson's unique and powerful contribution to the genre proving extremely popular in 2004, the idea of watching Jesus on film has suddenly become topical, and is, perhaps, an opportunity to grasp.

#78

Leaving Cert: A religious "X-Files" module about The Holy Grail, Turin Shroud, 666/Antichrist etc.

While in-depth Bible study may not always be an alluring prospect for young people, there are some religious topics that they will invariably respond to. Such areas may prove an effective gateway to further interest for those not religiously inclined. A Leaving Cert module containing a study of the following sort of material would at least prove engaging for young people:

- The Turin Shroud — is it a fake?
- Exorcists and Exorcisms — real life examples
- Stigmata — the history and nature of them
- 666/Antichrist — what does it say in Revelations?
- The Holy Grail — myth or actual relic?

An indication that such material has appeal for young people can be seen in the popularity of movies dealing with such subjects. *Stigmata, The Exorcist* and *The Omen* are three obvious ones — but even the phenomenally popular Indiana Jones involved quests for two Biblical relics: The Ark of the Covenant and The Holy Grail.

#79

Leaving Cert: If people had good knowledge of the Gospels they would find Mass and religion more relevant

All of Fr Jim Caffrey's contribution relates perfectly to this idea, so it is included here intact:

"I would love to see young people reading the Gospels using the method of *Lectio Divina*. The Gospels have the power to change their lives and by falling in love with Jesus Christ they will in turn reach out to the poor and needy. The starting point is to help them open the Bible and read the Gospel."

#80

Leaving Cert: Study the evidence that currently exists for the existence of Jesus and events in His life

The excellent book *Jesus: The Evidence* by Ian Wilson contains fascinating information about the proof that exists for believing in what Catholics believe. Might it serve as an excellent textbook for believers and sceptics alike?

#81

Leaving Cert: Teach a module about modern miracles and apparitions since Jesus' time

Young people are fascinated by the supernatural. Movies such as *The Sixth Sense* and *The Others,* dealing with ghosts, were among the most popular films of recent years. The stories of apparitions and miracles are not only fascinating — they are possibly real. Do we underestimate the power of such tales?

#82

Leaving Cert: Teach basics of world religions and compare with Catholicism

With the declining influence of the Church in Irish schools, and the growing numbers of people of other beliefs in Ireland, does learning about other belief systems represent a threat (as one contributor did) or an opportunity for the Catholic Church?

#83

Awareness of the lives of relevant saints who weren't always perfect — St Augustine, Matt Talbot etc.

Deirdre Manifold urges, "you do what you can to make Matt Talbot known to young people. He was a real hero who ought to appeal to all young people." In light of the drink problem in Ireland, this suggestion is certainly relevant. St Augustine is also ideal as a role model for young people who feel they have strayed far from the Church's teachings. Cardinal Connell says "he spent the years of his youth in the shallows until he heard God's voice calling him out into the deep". With many young people treading in the shallows today, at least Augustine is a saint they can identify with. We may find, as the teacher Elizabeth Lev reveals, "as we start the semester and talk about the martyrs' heroic resistance and unfaltering belief, they are fascinated". "Look at Francis of Assisi, St Vincent de Paul, Mother Teresa, the St Egidio community," Patsy McGarry reminds us, "spanning centuries yet doing the same thing. None had/have problems recruiting young followers to the Church/Christ."

#84

Educate about Church's history and its ability to get through crises and stand the test of time

"Before you apply to [the Gospel of St Matthew] the supposedly rational tests which you would apply to a newspaper report or a television documentary, imagine the chapters which describe the trial and Crucifixion of Christ set to music in Bach's *Saint Matthew Passion*. Consider the millions of people who, for the last 1900 years have recited the prayer (6:9-13), which begins "Our Father". Think of the old women in Stalin's Russia, when the men were too cowardly to profess their loyalty to the

Church, who stubbornly continued to chant the opening verses of the Sermon on the Mount in defiance of the KGB. 'Blessed are they that mourn for they shall be comforted'". — Wilson, 1985. The use of the word "crisis" referred to in this book's Introduction could sometimes be tempered by reference to the Church's ability to "endure the passage of time". One might especially consider and portray this particular country's rich history, spanning centuries of persecution without the abandonment of its faith, as grounds for optimism.

<h2 style="text-align:center">#85</h2>

<h2 style="text-align:center">Provide a simple explanation and Bible back up for controversial Church teachings</h2>

From contributions, we see a clear sense of anger at what many young people feel are rules made up by the Church.

"I believe," Barbara Johnston writes, "that young people see the teachings of the Church to be outdated. They are more outspoken and better educated. They are not afraid to ask the questions we only thought about. They ask why priests cannot get married, why are women second-class citizens in the Church, what gives the Church the right to dictate on contraception and many other questions that have never really been answered." Clearly, many young people seem to require better or clearer answers than the ones they are currently receiving or deciphering.

#86

Establish a special "youth ministry" for every young person at 16–17 to suit their interests, e.g. football/writing/voluntary work

Contributors have spoken about giving young people "space and responsibility". Many adults achieve this in the Church via various ministries, yet there is a vacuum of opportunity between altar-service and such roles during the teens, where many are coincidentally losing their interest. Fr Martin Tierney offers a "children's ministry" in his parish, as well an "Alpha Bible course", a ministry of welcome and a youth Mass. In offering different types of opportunity — other than just reading or singing in a choir — one obviously increases the chances of retaining young people. Youth ministries need not be limited to existing practices. By "thinking outside the box of the Mass", the definition of ministries could be widened to maximise opportunity for all talents and all parts of life. Young people could carry their faith —torches in their football team, as writers of conscience, or as human rights campaigners. What's important is that good deeds are done in Jesus' name, where people feel competent and stimulated.

#87

Have a special spiritual advisor for every young person who they contact almost anytime they need to

Kevin Doran speaks about "tapping into the real needs and heart wishes of young people, supporting them in their decision-making in a way which respects and enhances their freedom, rather than stifling it". He believes that "we need to find a way to make it part of the ministry of every parish community". This point can be linked with Treacy O'Connor's wish that the Church might be "*spiritual guides* for us, rather than preaching to us", and Seán O'Sullivan contention that "clergy should not be reluctant to act as spiritual directors".

#88

Give special book to young people, with useful prayers and contacts for times of need e.g. bereavement/exams

One contributor suggested the distribution of "a small booklet . . . with a list of aspirations and a little explanation on each," claiming that "a few short quotations from the Bible would make certain people think about religion". Perhaps the opportunity for this lies in its relevance to their daily lives and worries. If the booklet was to successfully "address some of their concerns", as Rev Paul Clayton-Lea considers vital, then it might even become a fixture in their schoolbags, wallets and handbags.

#89

Sanction an official Church blessing for cohabiting couples who officially declare intent to marry in Church

With weddings and rent prohibitively expensive, and the "living in sin" tag still being applied to cohabiting couples, can a compromise be reached?

"The God I know does not mind if you sleep with someone when you are in a committed relationship." How does one reconcile this young person's view with abstinence before marriage? In an age when *Sugar* magazine teaches its young teenage readers how to please their boyfriends via "good" oral sex technique, how realistic is it to expect virginity at marriage? For merely economic reasons alone, living together makes sense for more and more young couples, whose alternative is rent that absorbs up to 80 per cent of an average net monthly wage.

The Christian Community Bible tells us that at the time of Christ's conception, "engagements gave to the Jewish people practically every right of marriage, especially conjugal rights". In an age where casual sex is a greater danger to society than sex in a committed relationship — and this finds agreement with liberals as well as conservatives — might the Church find middle ground with such "conjugal rights" as part of a Church-sanctioned "engagement"?

#90

Set up a political party with young, educated candidates based on honesty, social issues and sound economics

The disillusionment and apathy of youth at election time is well documented. Much of this is related to a pattern of dishonesty, corruption, scandal and controversial government policies. However, the crowds of young people who took to the streets in anti-war protests bore testimony to their passion and a sign that they care — but often feel ignored. A new, well-backed political party, based on Christian values and driven by social issues and justice might be an opportune way to involve young people and religious in the same movement. Contributors Justin Barrett and Nora Bennis have attempted to do something similar on a small scale but, as Ronan Mullen points out, "there are plenty of committed Christians around: people skilled in business, management, communication, advertising, who, if brought on board, could make interesting things happen".

#91

Have a good church hall in every parish that can be used for youth groups, video/DVD screenings and activities

"Of course, for many . . . activities, a church hall is a necessity. I was surprised when I moved here to find that there was no hall attached to the Sacred Heart Church.

Apart from being used for church activities, a church or parish hall would obviate the need for meetings, i.e. active retirement group, historical society, etc., being held in public houses." — Ruth O'Sullivan

#92

"Wipe the slate clean" confession campaign to promote and make confession easier and less daunting

In his recent book, *The Healing Power of Confession*, Scott Hahn contends that confession has never been more relevant. Indeed, American studies have shown that almost half of US priests attend the sacrament twice or less in a year. Only by confessing our sins, Hahn contends, do we allow God to take them away. The words of Christ — from the Gospels to Sister Faustina's Divine Mercy messages — re-iterate the possibility of absolution through confession. Young people, who feel they are not observing Church rules, and thus stay away, are the group most relevant to the sacrament. They, most of all, need to be convinced that their mistakes, for which they are sorry, will not be judged in the confessional — but forgiven and forgotten.

#93

Highlight nature of tarot cards, psychics, etc. via contrast between new age practices and the authenticity of Christianity

It seems that anyone can become an agony aunt and give people advice on complex issues: from retired Eurovision contestants (Maxi in the *RTE Guide*) to lesbian ex-nuns (*Ask Anna* on RTE 1). Tarot card readings on TV advise people what house to buy or what relationship to enter. "What peculiar psychology is at work", Dick Ahlstrom writes (*Irish Times*, 30 October 2003), "that makes consumers rightly sceptical about extravagant claims made by product advertisers, but willing to pay big money for medical treatments involving crystals and long-distance cures? We live in a time when pseudoscience and mumbo jumbo are treated with the same sober gravity as evidence-based medicine and quantum mechanics."

The phenomenon of new-age practices has partly gained at the expense of religion, picking up people who describe themselves as "spiritual", but "not in a religious way".

How does the Church address the needs, which such practices obviously pander to? Leanne Faulkner recommends three themes for sermons:

1. Find out where you want to go with your life

2. Discover how to be a better person

3. How to find your vocation in life by listening to your inner self.

These may sound a little wishy-washy, but in essence, Christ gives people answers to these exact questions, especially if one substitutes "God" for "inner self" in (3) above. In moving into this territory, which so obviously fills a vacuum for so many people, the Church could entice some young people.

#94

Let young people know about suitable youth and voluntary groups and provide a free leaflet with contact details

Membership of groups is always a great way to intensify commitment to a cause, be it Liverpool Supporters Club or the Legion of Mary. Sr Malachy O'Farrell recommends the latter, as well as Youth 2000 which, she adds, "has branches all over". While Youth 2000's details are readily available at the Blessed Sacrament Chapel in Dublin, where they meet, not every young person will learn of their existence elsewhere. It would surely be fruitful for the membership of such youth groups if the Church were to provide their names, descriptions and contact details on a user-friendly leaflet.

#95

Set up special "youth pilgrimages" — visiting a holy place and surrounding area in a fun break with other young people

Father Hugh Hanley of the Twenty- and Thirtysome-things discusses the social needs of young people, "but they are also interested in retreats and pilgrimages", he says. "Pilgrimages", Mary Kenny says, "are absolutely vital." Having attended Lough Derg and seen the number of committed young people there who appeared to relish the experience, it is difficult to disagree that exposure to the culture, meaning and social aspect of pilgrimage is as potent for youth as it ever was. The Prior of Lough Derg, Richard Mohan, is best qualified to close this final thesis:

"Assuming there is commitment I believe that any kind of togetherness, community, belonging to a group of like-minded young people — this will strengthen the commitment. . . . I believe that if they can be brought in touch with 'Church' through some shared experience, probably a challenging one — the more authentic the better (for example a walk or fast or project or retreat or pilgrimage) — they may keep in touch through their peers."

The "New 95 Theses" in Brief: Seek and Youth Shall Find!

Of course, representing over 120 contributions via 95 ideas for a school questionnaire is one thing — trying to summarise the essence of these disparate suggestions is quite another. Yet, on close inspection, it is possible to classify them into four distinct categories:

1. Stimulation

Lack of stimulation was frequently referred to by contributors. This was usually in the context of mental stimulation, and seven areas suggested as potential remedy sources are listed below.

1. Mass

2. Motivation

3. Music

4. Movies

5. Media

6. Message

7. Mingling

In the main, bringing youth culture into the mix is seen as crucial.

2. Example

Approximately a quarter of suggested ideas touched on the notion that young people need appropriate inspiration from other people. This may come from the good example of others, the ability of people to testify to their faith and the immediacy of cultural heroes or from idols bearing witness to their Christian faith and/or ideals. The three main suggested sources of "example" can be effectively summarised thus:

1. Witnesses

2. Idols

3. Good example.

3. Engagement

According to contributors, young people need to be engaged in Church affairs if they are to commit to it. This means they must be invited, involved, interested and integrated. Conversely, the Church is called to:

1. Invite

2. Involve

3. Interest and

4. Integrate.

4. Knowledge

Finally, knowledge, or lack of it was cited as a problem in many forms. Three key potential sources were identified:

1. The Gospels

2. Adults

3. School.

Thus, in order to be attracted to the Church, one might conclude that young people need:

- **S**timulation
- **E**xample
- **E**ngagement and
- **K**nowledge.

Of course, taking the first letter of each word gives us the religious mnemonic: SEEK. *Matthew 7:7* quotes Jesus thus: "Ask and you will receive; seek and you will find; knock and the door will be opened. For everyone who asks receives; whoever seeks finds."

It would be nice to think that stimulation, good example, engagement and knowledge equates to the "seeking" that Jesus refers to. If nothing else, the mnemonic neatly summarises the views of concerned and consulted adults. But what of the people for whom this volume has been compiled? Part 3 looks at what young people have to say about it all.

Part 3

YOUTH RESPOND

INTRODUCTION

Of course, the 95 ideas presented in Parts 1 and 2 represent the thoughts of people who lie outside this book's target demographic. One of the advantages of this was the potential it offered to gauge the difference in perceptions between young people and those who make decisions for them. In order to do this a survey of young people's attitudes to the ideas was, of course, necessary.

A total of 446 students took part and the data allowed for robust statistical analysis by commitment levels to the Church, age group and geographical location.[1] It is worth noting that the Nielsen TV ratings, which fuel TV advertising business worth millions of euro a month in this country, rely on a much smaller panel size of approximately 330 12–18 year olds.

---

[1] Conclusions regarding gender can also be made, albeit with a relatively small sample.

Praise is due to the Religious Education teachers in each of the three schools involved, who meticulously guided their students through the questionnaires. The students are also to be praised for completing the daunting task of grading 95 ideas and rating their own commitment to the Church. What their efforts yielded makes for absorbing reading, and is useful in three particular contexts:

- As many of us believe, the Church needs to take young people "where they are", so it's useful to ascertain where that is.

- For want of a better way of putting it, we tend to tell young people "where to go" when it comes to the Church; however, it's not necessarily where they want to be. They are adolescents, after all! In knowing where they actually want to go, it may at least be possible to direct them to a mutually agreeable place.

- Those attempting to attract vocations in this country need to tap into the notoriously elusive and relatively cynical psyche of its teenagers.

The students of Swords (County Dublin), Athenry (County Galway), and Youghal (County Cork) have hopefully provided answers to many questions posed in these three contexts.

If nothing else — and excuse the lame mnemonic — it is a timely opportunity for some young people in this country to have a SAY about their church!

SAMPLES AND COMMITMENT

The following grid indicates the broad composition of the 446-pupil survey:

Table 1: Overall Composition of Respondents

Commitment	School			Total
	Swords	*Athenry*	*Youghal*	
0/1s	63	30	66	159
2/3s	77	24	121	222
4/5s	18	12	35	65
Mean commitment	2.0	2.8	2.3	2.2
All	158	66	222	446
11–14s	90	—	85	175
15+	62	66	135	263

Thus, respondents were classified according to how they rated their "commitment" to the Church (from 0 to 5), where 0 is "none" and 5 is "extremely committed".

This was the first task on the questionnaire and, along with "age", provided some interesting cross-tabs in later analysis.

For the purposes of the analysis, 11-14 inclusive and 15-18 inclusive (or 15+) were grouped. This provided two classifications much in keeping with First to Third Years (Junior Cert) and Fourth/Transition Year to Leaving Certificate classes. It also helped to keep Athenry results in one age section, as the questionnaires returned came only from students of 15 or over. The aforementioned Nielsen TV ratings panel sizes are just under 170 for both 11–14s and 15+, proving this survey's samples, of 175 and 263 respectively, to be more than robust.

In ascertaining the relationship between age and commitment, it was generally discovered that commitment tended to wane as age increased:

Table 2: Average Commitment by Age

Age	Swords	Athenry	Youghal
11/12	2.2	—	3.4
13	2.1	—	3.0
14	2.5	—	2.7
15	1.5	3.0	2.8
16	1.4	1.8	2.2
17/18	1.6	2.2	2.4

The slightly disconcerting fact to be drawn from the above is that, for both Swords and Youghal, commitment to the Church falls considerably (virtually by 30 per cent) from the age of entry to the age of departure. However, one can counter this with a positive: the new generation is entering school with about 40 per cent more commitment than those who are about to leave it. The challenge is to maintain — or even increase — the commitment levels of the 11/12s through the secondary system; preferences among the "Theses" may give us some clues how to do this.

Another negative/positive "combo" relates to 16-year-olds. For all three schools, this was the age where commitment was lowest. While this seemingly inevitable trough in commitment to the Church must be cause for concern, the subsequent growth in commitment for the

17/18s presents grounds for optimism. Furthermore, being able to specifically identify an age where commitment is weakest is no bad thing.

THE QUALITATIVE RESPONSE

While 446 students completed questionnaires, only about one in five replied to its final prompt, which asked them this book's central question, phrased slightly differently:

> "Do you have a good idea [for the Church to attract young people] yourself? Write it here in the space provided."

The answers (below) are classed according to how the students rated their "commitment" to the Church (from 0 to 5). While the intrinsic part of this section's research is quantitative, and contained further below, the quotations collected here serve as a "vox pop" of sorts and may indicate where some young people are at in relation to the Church:

Commitment of 5

"Stop making your sheets so long." (A)

Commitment of 4

"Good songs and good days out, e.g. Lough Derg." (S)

"Have Mass on Sunday at about 8:30 pm." (S)

"Have the Community totally involved in the works of the Church. Teach the relevance of faith in life." (S)

"Priests should be able to get married; this is an enormous factor as to why there is a great decline in application for priesthood." (Y)

"Do away with the idea of different religions and just try to lead a good life." (Y)

"Don't continue to make sermons so boring." (Y)

"Have a soundproof room developed into a crèche for smaller children." (Y)

"Mass in school to get people involved." (Y)

Commitment of 3

"Get the views of young people and see what they want." (S)

"A band singing. Happy, joyful place." (S)

"More lively/singing/modern Church." (S)

"Make Mass shorter with no singing hymns or talk during the middle." (S)

"Liven up the service!" (S)

"Make it more interesting." (S)

"Make Mass more exciting. People only go because they have to/because they feel they have to." (Y)

"There should be tea and sandwiches after Mass around once a month to encourage people to go to Mass." (Y)

"Food at Church." (Y)

"Make Mass shorter." (Y)

"Encourage talk about Ouija boards and Exorcism." (Y)

"Make Masses shorter." (Y)

"Group talks in schools and more talking with youths." (Y)

"Make the Mass shorter and more interesting." (Y)

"Singing at Mass less boring." (Y)

"Make religion less like brainwashing and slightly interesting." (Y)

Commitment of 2

"Sing all the primary school songs again." (S)

"Make Church less boring." (S)

"The Church needs to become more personal, focusing on the individual as part of a group." (S)

"Don't force people to pray." (S)

"Be more fun, enjoyable, less strict, and get rid of # 69 (thesis relating to text number to God)." (S)

"Make Mass about 20 minutes long and less of the readings they say at every Mass." (A)

"Shorter Mass times; make them more interesting and more than two Mass times on a Sunday." (A)

"More young people involved in music in the Church." (A)

"Less about the Bible — more about our lives." (A)

"Have a Church soccer team for children and the priest should be manager." (Y)

"The Church should provide less authority and more guidance to people." (Y)

"Make a fast musical Mass; make Mass like the black people's Mass." (Y)

"Let priests have families." (Y)

"Set up a holy Church in school for students and have a priest come in room every certain day." (Y)

"Get more young people involved." (Y)

Commitment of 1

"Make it like the American Churches." (S)

"Make the Church modern." (S)

"Don't just make it about God. Teach more everyday things that happen to everyone." (S)

"Make it more fun. Make it shorter." (S)

"Bring in women priests." (S)

"Make religion fun." (S)

"A Church soccer team." (Y)

"I think everybody shouldn't listen to priests and the Bible; they should make up their own minds about God." (Y)

"If you think a lot of these topics are relevant to young people, you're wrong. Please be more realistic." (Y)

"Make Church more fun and interesting." (Y)

"It's too late for the Church to come back so I wouldn't bother trying." (Y)

"Layout surveys better/it was so boring!!" (Y)

"Play metal music at Mass or some other music young people will like, that's not boring." (Y)

"Provide food at Mass." (Y)

Commitment of 0/No rating given:

"Are u joking?" (S)

"Serve pizza during Mass — lots will go then." (S)

"Have a special Mass for young people and make it more interesting with songs and telling stories." (S)

"Make the church like a disco and have lots of music made by the young people. Have no adults." (S)

"More fun and younger priests." (S)

"Young people should not be told what to believe. They should make their own choices." (S)

"Less emphasis on God and more on self-development — both physical and mental." (A)

"Shorter Masses — leave out singing." (A)

"Have discos in Mass." (A)

"Don't baptise Christians until they're over 12 and old enough to make their own decision." (Y)

"Stop pushing the Church, it's dead, get over it!" (Y)

Even from such throwaway remarks, some common threads are evident:

- Though asked a question about the Church, many respondents replied with suggestions about Mass, implying an interchangeable association between the two: the quality of the Mass is clearly equated with the state of the Church as a whole

- Mass is too long, and too serious, many feel; an injection of fun and energy is clearly desired

- Some credit for the intelligence and free will of teenagers is being demanded

- The existence of a thin line between the Church's hands-on involvement at ground level and its interference in people's lives is also quite clearly stated.

Further generalisations are possible when we focus on the quantitative results presented next.

METHODOLOGY AND MEASUREMENT

On the distributed questionnaires, all 95 suggested ideas were presented on both sides of one page for students to grade. One tick denoted a "good idea"; two ticks indicated a "very good idea". Uncertainty or a "bad idea" was expressed by no mark.

As mentioned earlier, the order of the theses was based solely on them fitting on one page! Thus, the 31 longest-worded ideas were included on one side, with two columns of (32) shorter theses on the other. The aesthetics of the page was considered important, and while one student did call for a better layout, labelling the survey "boring", the vast majority of questionnaires were filled out thoroughly and neatly.

In assessing which were the most (and least) popular ideas, three distinct measurements were used:

- With two ticks being awarded for a very good idea, the maximum number of ticks possible for each thesis is twice the number of students in the sample. The percentage of the maximum possible ticks obtained (MAX) was this study's preferred measurement of the popularity of a thesis, as it took "very good" and "good" marks into account, and weighted "very good" appropriately.

- To assess which ideas were most likely to meet with very positive responses, one might wish to assess the "very good" ticks as a proportion of the total possible (VG) only. This standard was used more sparingly than MAX, but it is arguably as useful a gauge of popularity.

- Finally, if one wants to consider an idea's general acceptance level it may be sufficient to note how many respondents consider it either good or very good (G+VG). This "catch-all" measure ignores degrees of acceptability, providing encouragingly high figures compared to B and C, so it's more suitable to quote for those who wish to say the churches are half full!

To illustrate briefly: with a sample of 100, each idea has the potential to attract a maximum of 200 ticks. A thesis with 30 "very good" ratings and 40 "good" ratings will achieve the following measures:

MAX = (30 × 2) + (40 × 1) as a % of 200 = 50%
VG = 30 as a % of 100 = 30%
G+VG = 30 + 40 as a % of 100 = 70%

While there is a clear difference between the three measurements of the same thesis, above, it is the relative ranking of each thesis that is of primary concern to this study — and the good news is that a remarkably uniform pattern emerges when the theses are ranked in order of popularity.[2] To begin, the 20 ideas which proved most (and least) popular are presented below:

---

[2] In the list of ideas below, some have been shortened — or get shortened further as they are used repeatedly; for full wordings, see Part 3.

	MAX Top 20 Overall	
No.	*Thesis/Key Word(s)*	*%*
1	#28 Use more humour	71
2	#15 Married priests	69
3	#47 Clamp down on child abuse	65
4	#20 Suicide support and advice	62
5	#14 Women priests	61
6	#5 Change Mass dramatically	55
=7	#6 Happy vibe at Mass/up-tempo liturgy	53
=7	#91 Church hall for activities	53
=7	#60 Non-judgemental reaction to teen pregnancy	53
=10	#65 Adapt modern songs for Mass	52
=10	#57 Speak language of youth	52
=10	#48 Training for priests	52
=10	#10 Short motivational sermon	52
=10	#1 Let youth air views and listen	52
15	#46 Explain Vatican wealth	51
16	#8 Lots more singing and music	50
=17	#67 Child sponsorship in schools	49
=17	#49 Younger, approachable priests	49
19	#3 Church active in the community	47
=20	#68 Blessing oneself habitually	46
=20	#92 Wipe slate clean confession campaign	46

	MAX Bottom 10 Overall	
No.	*Thesis/Key Word(s)*	*%*
1	#30 End money racket at Communions, etc.	19
2	#51 Youth bearing witness to their faith	23
3	#59 Charitable use of SSIAs	24
=4	#33 Sunday school	25
=4	#21 Families to pray together	25
=4	#69 Text messages to "God" number	25
=4	#12 Promote suitable books/mags	25
=4	#72 Alternatives to materialism	25
9	#55 Teach daily prayer routine	26
10	#82 Teach about other religions	27

When presented in terms of "very good" ideas only, the Top 20 looks like this:

	VG Top 20 Overall	
No.	*Thesis/Key Word(s)*	*%*
1	#28 Use more humour	56
2	#15 Married priests	54
3	#47 Clamp down on child abuse	50
4	#14 Women priests	46
5	#20 Suicide support and advice	42
6	#5 Change Mass dramatically	38
7	#6 Happy vibe at Mass/up-tempo liturgy	37
8	#91 Church hall for activities	35
=8	#46 Explain Vatican wealth	35
10	#10 Short motivational sermon	34

11	#8 Lots more music and singing at Mass	33
12	#65 Adapt modern songs for Mass	31
13	#48 Training for priests	30
=14	#60 Non-judgemental reaction to teen pregnancy	29
=14	#17 Less anti-gay rhetoric	29
=16	#77 Study spiritual movies	28
=16	#73 Special Mass times for youth	28
=18	#57 Speak language of youth	27
=18	#16 Dating agency for Catholics	27
=18	#49 Younger, approachable priests	27

And the bottom 10 is slightly different too:

	VG Bottom 10 Overall	
No.	*Thesis/Key Word(s)*	*%*
=1	#21 Families to pray together	8
=1	#51 Youth bearing witness to their faith	8
3	#22 Adults as witnesses to their faith	9
=4	#84 Teach Church history	10
=4	#72 Alternatives to materialism	10
=6	#82 Teach about other religions	11
=6	#55 Teach daily prayer routine	11
=6	#30 End money racket at Communions etc.	11
=6	#12 Promote suitable books/mags	11
10	#82 Teach about other religions	12

G+VG Top 20 Overall		
No.	*Thesis/Key Word(s)*	*%*
1	#28 Use more humour	86
2	#15 Married priests	85
3	#3 Suicide support and advice	82
4	#47 Clamp down on child abuse	81
5	#1 Let youth air views and listen	78
6	#57 Speak language of youth	77
=7	#14 Women priests	76
=7	#60 Non-judgemental reaction to teen pregnancy	76
=9	#65 Adapt modern songs for Mass	73
=9	#48 Training for priests	73
=11	#5 Change Mass dramatically	72
=11	#67 Child sponsorship in schools	72
13	#91 Church hall for activities	71
=14	#6 Happy vibe at Mass/up-tempo liturgy	70
=14	#10 Short motivational sermon	70
=14	#49 Younger, approachable priests	70
=17	#3 Church active in the community	68
=17	#46 Explain Vatican wealth	68
=17	#92 Wipe slate clean confession campaign	68
=20	#68 Blessing oneself habitually	66
=20	#44 Good speakers at mass	66

	G+VG Bottom 10 Overall	
No.	*Thesis/Key Word(s)*	*%*
1	#30 End money racket at Communions etc.	28
2	#59 Charitable use of SSIAs	33
3	#69 Text messages to 'God' number	35
=4	#51 Youth bearing witness to their faith	37
=4	#33 Sunday school	37
6	#12 Promote suitable books/mags	39
=7	#76 Catholicism a L. Cert subject	41
=7	#55 Teach daily prayer routine	41
=7	#36 Weekend youth retreats	41
=10	#21 Families to pray together	42
=10	#45 Special Youth Masses	42

Whether we assess by the MAX or VG methods outlined above, the order of preference is almost exactly the same, with only the order of "suicide support and advice" and "women priests" at fourth and fifth of the Top 8 different.

We can't claim to be surprised that "married priests", "women priests" and "child abuse" feature in the final Top 6. That all were eclipsed by the suggestion of clergy cracking a few jokes might raise some eyebrows, however. Call it the *Father Ted* factor or something else, but young people certainly don't see humour as a "no go" area for the Church, with only 1 in 7 not in support of the concept. Indeed, if one were to marry Thesis 28 with Thesis 48, one might find some solutions to this book's quest: effective training for priests in how to endear oneself to one's audience via humour.

Some alarm may be expressed at the high position of "suicide support and advice" on the list; clearly, it's a very pertinent issue for young people, particularly the 15+ age group, where the suggestion was top of the poll in Athenry — 93 per cent of the Galwegians considered advice and support around the suicide issue by the Church to be a good idea, with half of these describing it as a "very good" idea.

When we look at overall approval ratings (G+VG), allowing young people to air their views and have them listened to, and the similar "speaking the language of youth" theses were among the Top 6, while 21 theses in all were supported by at least two in three students (66 per cent).

In terms of unpopular ideas, the concept of curbing the monetary excesses of Communions and other Church occasions did not go down too well, with the idea attracting a mere 19 per cent of the maximum score possible, and only 11 per cent calling it a very good idea. While the former rating was the worst of all 95 theses, the latter was only joint sixth worst. Encouraging families to pray together and getting people of any age to bear witness to their faith secured the fewest number of "very good" ratings.

The attractiveness of each idea fell considerably from the 11–14 group to the 15+ age-group, where a mere 5 per cent approved strongly of anyone bearing witness to their faith, and only 4 per cent found praying with one's family particularly appealing.

Somewhat ironically, these three theses are among those most suggested by contributors, namely at No. 3

(adults bearing witness), No. 5 (young people bearing witness) and No. 13 (families praying together) in the Top 20 list.

This anomaly can be interpreted to mean one of several things:

- Some adults are completely out of touch with young people and their needs

- Young people don't know what's good for them

- Neither side has all the answers, and most self-conscious teenagers will naturally rebel against and even cringe at outward expressions of religious faith.

The overall Top 10s and Top 20s are useful for drawing general conclusions, naturally, and more exhaustive conclusions can be established by assessing the full results for all 95 Theses, listed in Appendix A. However, less painful analysis continues below, with more Top 10 and Top 20 treatment — this time by age group, area and commitment. In assessing the results of these subsections, we become aware that making the Church attractive to young people requires different approaches with different groups.

Age Groups

General differences between the 11–14s and 15–18s are borne out by their expressed preferences in the survey. The older group are far less likely to refer to an idea as "very good", and their Top 10 preferences prefer suicide support and advice to women priests, and include deal-

ing with teenage pregnancy, unlike their young counterparts.

The differences are hardly monumental, however:
the theses in their respective Top 6s are exactly the
same. It is essentially the variation in enthusiasm that
differentiates the two groups, which of course, is high-
lighted by the drop in commitment by age discussed
above. The 76 per cent who think that humour is a very
good idea before 15 becomes 42 per cent for 15 and over,
for example. Blessing of the home is rated as a "very
good" idea by a mere 5 per cent of the older group compared to 18 per cent of 11–14s. In fact, one has to look
extremely hard to find any thesis which finds most fervour among those 15 and over.

There is one notable exception: confirmation at a
later age received more "two-tick" ratings for the 15+
group, and significantly more than any thesis on the second half of the questionnaire page. Perhaps this repre-
sents an opportunity for the Church to improve commitment at an age (16) where it suffers a notable dip.

	MAX Top 10 — 11–14s	
No.	*Thesis/Key Word(s)*	*%*
1	#28 Use more humour	69
2	#15 Married priests	68
3	#47 Clamp down on child abuse	66
4	#14 Women priests	65
5	#20 Suicide support and advice	62
6	#5 Change Mass dramatically	58
7	#57 Speak language of youth	57
8	#1 Let youth air views and listen	56
9	#8 Lots more singing and music	55
10	#3 Church active in the community	54

	MAX Top 10 — 15+	
No.	*Thesis/Key Word(s)*	*%*
1	#15 Married priests	64
2	#28 Use more humour	63
3	#47 Clamp down on child abuse	57
4	#20 Suicide support and advice	56
=5	#14 Women priests	53
=5	#5 Change Mass dramatically	53
7	#1 Let youth air views and listen	49
8	#48 Training for priests	48
=9	#8 Lots more singing and music	46
=9	#10 Short motivational sermon	46
=9	#60 Non-judgemental reaction to teen pregnancy	46

No.	VG Top 10 — 15+ Thesis/Key Word(s)	%
1	#15 Married priests	46
2	#28 Use more humour	42
3	#47 Clamp down on child abuse	40
4	#14 Women priests	38
5	#20 Suicide support and advice	35
6	#5 Change Mass dramatically	34
7	#6 Happy vibe at Mass/up-tempo liturgy	29
8	#46 Explain Vatican wealth	27
=9	#8 Lots more music and singing at Mass	26
=9	#64 Confirmation at 16/17	26

No.	VG Top 10 — 11–14s Thesis/Key Word(s)	%
1	#28 Use more humour	76
2	#15 Married priests	67
3	#47 Clamp down on child abuse	63
4	#14 Women priests	58
5	#20 Suicide support and advice	53
6	#57 Speak language of youth	49
7	#10 Short motivational sermon	47
8	#46 Explain Vatican wealth	46
=9	#5 Change Mass dramatically	45
=9	#8 Lots more music and singing at Mass	45

Different Places

Differences between the three schools used in the survey cannot be used to make any sweeping statements about location — each school's respondents are decidedly different. Youghal is an all-male school, Swords is mixed and all Athenry questionnaires came from the 15+ group. Thus, comparisons between Swords and Youghal may tell us more about gender than geography, and Athenry's results are best compared to the overall 15+ results to assess if there is any "Galway effect".

Still, there is a mere 1 percentage point difference between the approval rating for "using humour more" among the three schools, indicating what the results generally show us — regardless of gender, age or commitment, there is a remarkable consistency to results involving the Top 5 or 6 theses. Not surprisingly, however, the mixed school has a greater taste for theses involving songs, music and happy vibes. The males in Youghal preferred theses regarding explanations about Church policy or action, such as providing better training for priests or a Church hall for activities.

Athenry's key difference with other schools is its placing of "suicide support and advice" at the top of the pile compared to fourth for 15+ students overall.

MAX Top 10 — Swords		
No.	Thesis/Key Word(s)	%
1	#28 Use more humour	75
2	#15 Married priests	72
3	#47 Clamp down on child abuse	70
3	#14 Women priests	70
5	#20 Suicide support and advice	63
6	#6 Happy vibe at Mass/up-tempo liturgy	62
7	#8 Lots more music and singing at Mass	61
8	#57 Speak language of youth	58
=9	#48 Training for priests	57
=9	#65 Adapt modern songs for Mass	57

MAX Top 10 — Athenry		
No.	Thesis/Key Word(s)	%
1	#20 Suicide support and advice	69
2	#15 Married priests	64
=3	#28 Use more humour	61
=3	#47 Clamp down on child abuse	61
5	#10 Short motivational sermon	58
6	#6 Happy vibe at Mass/up-tempo liturgy	57
7	#8 Lots more music and singing at Mass	55
8	#57 Speak language of youth	54
=9	#48 Training for priests	52
=9	#65 Adapt modern songs for Mass	52

	MAX Top 10 — Youghal	
No.	*Thesis/Key Word(s)*	*%*
1	#28 Use more humour	72
2	#15 Married priests	69
3	#47 Clamp down on child abuse	63
4	#14 Women priests	62
5	#5 Change Mass dramatically	58
6	#1 Let youth air views and listen	54
7	#91 Church hall for activities	53
=8	#57 Speak language of youth	52
=8	#60 Non-judgemental reaction to teen pregnancy	52
=10	#46 Explain Vatican wealth	51
=10	#10 Short motivational sermon	51
=10	#48 Training for priests	51

	G+VG Top10 — Swords	
No.	*Thesis/Key Word(s)*	*%*
=1	#60 Non-judgemental reaction to teen pregnancy	89
=1	#15 Married priests	89
=1	#14 Women priests	89
4	#28 Use more humour	87
5	#47 Clamp down on child abuse	86
=6	#92 Wipe slate clean confession campaign	85
=6	#20 Suicide support and advice	85
=8	#91 Church hall for activities	80
=8	#65 Adapt modern songs for Mass	80
=8	#49 Younger, approachable priests	80

	G+VG Top 10 — Athenry	
No.	*Thesis/Key Word(s)*	*%*
1	#20 Suicide support and advice	93
2	#28 Use more humour	86
3	#10 Short motivational sermon	83
=4	#67 Child sponsorship in schools	81
=4	#1 Let youth air views and listen	81
=6	#65 Adapt modern songs for Mass	78
=6	#47 Clamp down on child abuse	78
=6	#15 Married priests	78
9	#8 Lots more music and singing at Mass	75
10	#5 Change Mass dramatically	71

	G+VG Top 10 — Youghal	
No.	*Thesis/Key Word(s)*	*%*
1	#28 Use more humour	86
2	#15 Married priests	84
3	#1 Let youth air views and listen	79
4	#14 Women priests	78
5	#47 Clamp down on child abuse	77
6	#20 Suicide support and advice	76
7	#5 Change Mass dramatically	74
=8	#57 Speak language of youth	72
=8	#48 Training for priests	72
10	#60 Non-judgemental reaction to teen pregnancy	70

Commitment Type

Perhaps the analysis which carries most weight here is that relating to commitment groupings. Knowing what "does it" for young people with different levels of commitment is crucial for the Church, and the discrepancies evident in the results warn us not to tar the 0/1s with the same brush as the 4/5s. Using humour, for instance, is the clear No. 1 suggestion as far as 0–3s are concerned, yet the concept only ranks fourth for 4/5s, whose choices are somewhat more specific and theoretical.

The general trend is that enthusiasm for ideas rises substantially with commitment; the average percentage of "very good" ratings for a thesis is 16 per cent for 0/1s, 22 per cent for 2/3s and 27 per cent for 4/5s.

In cases such as pilgrimages, prayer books and knowledge-based ideas like learning about Church history, the Gospels and miracles and apparitions, approval ratings are markedly higher for 4/5s. Among the potential "Catholicism syllabus" suggestions, only the idea of studying movies with religious or spiritual themes appealed more to 0/1s than other commitment groupings. This idea was just outside the Top Ten for 0/1s. Elsewhere, 0/1s were clearly most enthusiastic about only one other idea: Confirmation at 16/17. Any plan to attract greater commitment among those with very little might note the relatively big impact of these ideas.

Conversely, when dealing with young people who have voluntarily come to Mass or a retreat, a different, more expansive set of tools can be used. Among the theses with the greatest gap between 4/5s and 0/1s were those recommending "Sunday as a special day for God", "Sunday school", "Stations of the Cross" and the notion that one can simultaneously be Christian and "cool".

The 2/3s were most likely to demand adjustments to the Mass. Perhaps this is because they have enough commitment to the Church to attend, but enough reservations to seek change. They call for "changing Mass drastically", "shorter sermons", "women priests", and recommendations about Mass concerning suitable TV, films and music more than any other group.

Care, of course, has to be taken to keep the 4/5s where they are in terms of their strong commitment. Providing "quiet time" at Masses, adapting modern songs for use at Mass, and letting young people air their views apparently best does this.

	MAX Top 10 — 0/1 Group	
No.	*Thesis/Key Word(s)*	*%*
=1	#28 Use more humour	70
=1	#15 Married priests	70
3	#14 Women priests	63
4	#47 Clamp down on child abuse	62
=5	#5 Change Mass dramatically	55
=5	#20 Suicide support and advice	55
=7	#91 Church hall for activities	49
=7	#65 Adapt modern songs for Mass	49
=9	#1 Let youth air views and listen	48
=9	#10 Short motivational sermon	48
=9	#48 Training for priests	48

	MAX Top 10 — 2/3 Group	
No.	*Thesis/Key Word(s)*	*%*
1	#28 Use more humour	76
2	#15 Married priests	69
3	#47 Clamp down on child abuse	67
=4	#20 Suicide support and advice	65
=4	#14 Women priests	65
=6	#68 Blessing oneself habitually	63
=	#60 Non-judgemental reaction to teen pregnancy	63
8	#57 Speak language of youth	62
=9	#67 Child sponsorship in schools	61
=9	#6 Happy vibe at Mass/up-tempo liturgy	61

	MAX Top 10 — 4/5 Group	
No.	*Thesis/Key Word(s)*	*%*
=1	#47 Clamp down on child abuse	70
=1	#15 Married priests	70
3	#20 Suicide support and advice	68
4	#28 Use more humour	65
5	#68 Blessing oneself habitually	62
=6	#14 Women priests	61
=6	#1 Let youth air views and listen	61
=8	#9 Time for quiet reflection at Mass	59
=8	#65 Adapt modern songs for Mass	59
=10	#60 Non-judgemental reaction to teen pregnancy	58
=10	#67 Child sponsorship in schools	58

	VG Top 10 — 0/1 Group	
No.	*Thesis/Key Word(s)*	*%*
=1	#28 Use more humour	49
=1	#15 Married priests	49
3	#47 Clamp down on child abuse	43
4	#14 Women priests	39
=5	#20 Suicide support and advice	34
=5	#5 Change Mass dramatically	34
7	#91 Church hall for activities	33
8	#8 Lots more singing and music at Mass	30
9	#64 Confirmation at 16/17	29
10	#10 Short motivational sermon	28

	VG Top 10 — 2/3 Group	
No.	*Thesis/Key Word(s)*	*%*
1	#28 Use more humour	63
2	#15 Married priests	56
3	#47 Clamp down on child abuse	52
4	#14 Women priests	51
5	#20 Suicide support and advice	45
6	#6 Happy vibe at Mass/up-tempo liturgy	44
7	#5 Change Mass dramatically	42
=8	#10 Short motivational sermon	38
=8	#46 Explain Vatican wealth	38
10	#91 Church hall for activities	37

	VG Top 10 — 4/5 Group	
No.	*Thesis/Key Word(s)*	*%*
=1	#47 Clamp down on child abuse	60
=1	#15 Married priests	60
3	#68 Blessing oneself habitually	53
=4	#28 Use more humour	52
=4	#20 Suicide support and advice	52
6	#14 Women priests	48
=7	#60 Non-judgemental reaction to teen pregnancy	43
=7	#46 Explain Vatican wealth	43
=9	#6 Happy vibe at Mass/up-tempo liturgy	40
=9	#95 Special youth pilgrimages	40

Where is the Common Ground?

So where is the common ground between this book's contributors and the young people this book is for? In this respect, the adults "got it right". Their top suggestion (getting young people to air their views and listening to them) is the winner on points when one assesses common preferences. It featured at joint tenth in the young people's Top 20.

	Top 20 Suggested Ideas (from Part 1)	
No.	*Thesis/Key Word(s)*	*%*
1	#1 Let youth air views and listen	17
2	#56 Make sure the basics are known	14
3	#22 Adults as witnesses to their faith	11
4	#18 Encourage youth to do voluntary work	10
5	#3 Church active in the community	8
=5	#43 Young people more involved	8
=5	#51 Youth bearing witness to their faith	8
=5	#76 Catholicism as a course of study	8
9	#6 Happy vibe at Mass/up-tempo liturgy	7
=10	#15 Married priests	6
=10	#35 Social groups for young Christians	6
=10	#83 Educate re lives of the saints	6
=13	#4 Small support groups for young people	5
=13	#8 Lots more music and singing at Mass	5
=13	#21 Families to pray together	5
=13	#36 Youth-based retreats	5
=13	#34 Special Church groups for teenagers	5
=13	#50 Redefine religion as good deeds etc.	5
=13	#85 Explain controversial teachings	5
=13	#95 Special youth pilgrimages	5

"Married priests" come next, followed by "creating a happy vibe at Mass", and "lots more singing and music at Mass". One can picture this compromise scenario: a Gospel choir thumping out "Oh Happy Day" while the priest, his wife and children listen to a young person giving a sermon based on his views of the Church. Perhaps this is not the ideal solution: a fifth thesis — the Church becoming more active in the Community — is also strongly suggested by both groups, for instance. Yet, with only five theses in common, the Church should certainly note anything that is mutually desirable.

Let's Be Realistic . . .

A career guidance teacher I had in secondary school once asked a classmate what he would like to do after school. "Medicine," he replied. "Come on, let's be realistic!" the teacher exclaimed. It is possibly unfair to ask young people what they would like if we subsequently dismiss it as unrealistic, but many theses are unlikely to be implemented, even in the lifetime of the young people who have voted in big numbers for them. If we look only at ideas that could readily be implemented, a rather different but interesting set of Theses rise to the top.

We see huge approval ratings of about 70% for four specific ideas that could be put into action with a little initiative and imagination.

	Top 10 "Realistic" Theses	MAX	VG	G+V G
No.	*Thesis/Key Word(s)*	%	%	%
1	#65 Adapt modern songs for Mass	52	31	73
2	#46 Explain Vatican wealth	51	35	68
3	#67 Child sponsorship in schools	49	26	72
4	#92 Wipe slate clean confession campaign	46	25	68
5	#77 Study spiritual movies	45	28	62
6	#70 Special Mass times for young people	44	22	61
7	#24 Explain Church purpose and structure	43	22	63
=8	#86 Youth ministry for everyone at 16/17	42	23	61
=8	#9 Time for quiet reflection at Mass	42	19	64
10	#88 Book with contacts for times of need	40	21	59
10	#64 Confirmation at 16/17	40	25	54

- The benefits to society of establishing a child sponsorship campaign from primary school age onwards could be huge, especially in terms of raising awareness of developing countries and our responsibilities to them.

- Re-inventing confession gets a decisive thumbs-up also. There is always the "Mary Magdalene" factor to draw on for the Church — it is one institution that forgives sinners unconditionally, no matter what their past, and that message is most powerfully realised in the sacrament of penance. However, portrayals of the Church as dogmatic and judgemental hardly encourage youth to confess their darkest moments in an equally dark confessional. Perhaps this is why the idea of an actual campaign that emphasises the unconditional forgiveness, which is such a part of devotions like the Divine Mercy, is so popular.

- The Vatican's vast wealth and the Church's hierarchical structure require explanation, according to 68 per cent and 63 per cent of the respondents.

- More than any other "specific" thesis, however, students loved the idea of adapting modern songs for Mass. This idea found favour with 80 per cent of Swords students and 73 per cent overall. Perhaps this means a rethink in terms of the songs that are currently being peddled on our altars and from choirstalls. The thesis referred to "modern songs that young people like". At present, do we actually have any proof that young people like the songs of praise that are currently used? Has anybody asked? Perhaps it's time to consider if singing the beautiful refrain from Jeff Buckley's "Hallelujah" — a song that is definitely liked by young people — is preferable to standing silent while a folk group sing a song we've never heard before. Other suggestions of songs that could be "adaptable" to suit a Church context include "Shackles" by Mary Mary, "Spirit in the Sky" by

Norman Greenbaum, "I Still Haven't Found What I'm Looking For" by U2 and "The Cross" by Prince.

We have seen two out of the three best-supported ideas related to the alleviation of poverty, if we consider the second part of the "Vatican wealth" thesis — potential sale of its treasures to aid the poor.

Another combination evident elsewhere in the Top 10 is where Confirmation and a youth ministry are individually advocated for 16/17-year-olds. Approval was as high as 58 per cent in Swords, and 54 per cent overall for the Confirmation idea, which was encouragingly most in favour with those claiming the lowest commitment to the Church: 35 per cent of Youghal students with low commitment thought it was a "very good" idea, which was more than twice the average for this demographic.

The youth ministry idea was approved by two in three students in Swords, with 11–14s in general far more supportive of the notion. The relative success of both ideas might provide food for thought as to whether they could be combined in a Transition Year or post-Junior Cert setting.

Conclusions: A Blueprint for the Future

For a general plan, one might simply propose that young people SEEK (and Youth Shall Find). It's certainly valid to say that young people need:

- Stimulation

- Example

- Engagement and

- Knowledge.

When we analyse young people's questionnaires closely, we see that Stimulation ideas were quoted almost 70% more than Knowledge-based ideas and 27% more than Engagement theses. Knowledge may rank higher in Maynooth and All Hallows, but it's merely a means to an end for Irish youth — and that end is Stimulation. If I were to write for a tabloid, I might summarise by saying that "Mass is boring for young people", but I prefer to say that "if young people are offered greater stimulation, they will stay involved with the Church".

While the 95 Theses put forward in Part 2 are appealing to young people at some level, not all are realistic for an action plan; some popular ideas, such as "women" and "married priests" may never happen. Thus, any blueprint for 2004 onwards must merely note their popularity for another day — another Pope, perhaps — and move on. Similarly, the least popular theses must be acknowledged by omission from such a plan. If young people bearing witness to their faith and learning about other religions are among the least popular ideas, why force them on an already disillusioned generation?

So what conclusions can be drawn from all of this? There is certainly enough consistency in the statistically robust survey results to safely recommend some ideas. If an eight-point plan were to be left on the Cardinal's table, this would be my submission based on the book's contents:

1. Laughter appears to be the best medicine for a young congregation with an ailing faith. Training priests to use humour effectively might make priests, their sermons and, ultimately, their message far more popular.

2. One can also confidently advise the Church to be a crutch for those afflicted or likely to be affected by suicide or unwanted pregnancy. If the clergy can't be funny, they can certainly "be there" for the dark moments when others might lack the will or compassion to help.

3. The child abuse issue is very much to the forefront of young people's minds, and possibly will be until a very firm stance is more evident and/or abuse claims, valid *and* false, are responsibly reported.

4. There is still a place for confession: all it appears to need is a campaign concerning its unconditional forgiveness and some modernisation.

5. Around 16 years of age, commitment to the Church takes a noticeable dive. By offering Confirmation and special youth ministries to each young person at that age, some of the "rot" might be stopped at source.

6. Adults have lamented a serious lack of knowledge in Biblical matters and basic theology among young people. With young people very disinterested in "other religions", and apparently unenlightened by the current syllabus, scope certainly exists for Catholicism to be introduced as a Leaving Certificate

subject. The following topics, all of which obtained greater than 50 per cent approval from students, could be considered for inclusion:

o Movies with religious themes

o The Turin Shroud, the Holy Grail, Revelations, etc.

o Evidence that supports the life of Jesus Christ

o The lives of saints who weren't always perfect.

7. Drastic change is called for around the issue of Mass. Contributors proposed several solutions, and some of these were among the most popular with respondents:

o Special Mass times for young people

o A happier, up-tempo liturgy with "quiet time" too

o Church songs to be adapted — sometimes a little liberally — from suitable modern songs that young people actually like

o Sermons that can't entertain should be short. An injection of humour is obviously preferable.

8. Finally, and appropriately, one can say something this book proves conclusively: young people have strong voices and equally strong opinions. It might (positively) surprise the Church to see the benefits of casting out a little deeper and actually listening to them.

APPENDIX A: MAIN SURVEY RESULTS*

Thesis #	SW	ATH	YGH	ALL	o/1s	2/3s	4/5s	15+	14–	ALL
	Max	Max	Max	Max	Max	Max	Max	Max	Max	G+VG
1	48	57	54	52	48	53	54	49	56	78
2	36	33	36	36	29	37	39	24	31	56
3	52	41	46	47	39	51	48	40	54	69
4	37	28	29	32	27	33	35	25	32	47
5	53	50	58	55	55	59	49	53	58	72
6	62	48	49	53	44	60	56	46	50	70
7	47	42	45	45	43	48	44	41	52	65
8	61	51	41	50	48	51	51	44	55	66
9	49	40	37	42	35	42	47	37	45	64

* For a full set of statistical tables containing results of the survey, please contact the author at project2004ad@hotmail.com.

Thesis #	SW Max	ATH Max	YGH Max	ALL Max	0/1s Max	2/3s Max	4/5s Max	15+ Max	14- Max	ALL G+VG
10	51	58	51	52	48	56	54	46	47	70
11	30	22	29	28	29	30	27	24	31	43
12	29	17	24	25	22	25	25	18	28	39
13	41	30	34	36	28	38	37	28	39	54
14	70	35	62	61	63	66	60	53	65	76
15	72	64	69	69	70	69	69	64	68	85
16	35	23	45	38	39	40	34	32	43	49
17	58	41	37	45	41	47	40	36	43	61
18	41	39	34	37	31	38	41	32	34	56
19	40	32	33	35	30	38	35	30	36	55
20	63	69	59	62	55	65	62	56	62	82
21	28	20	25	25	23	26	26	20	39	42
22	33	23	28	29	25	29	31	23	34	49

Thesis #	SW Max	ATH Max	YGH Max	ALL Max	0/1s Max	2/3s Max	4/5s Max	15+ Max	14- Max	ALL G+VG
23	47	28	39	40	31	42	40	29	45	59
24	47	39	41	43	37	44	48	39	46	63
25	39	33	33	35	30	36	36	27	35	55
26	40	31	33	35	31	34	39	26	39	50
27	36	29	28	31	23	30	41	25	31	47
28	75	61	72	71	70	76	69	63	69	86
29	32	15	28	27	22	30	30	22	30	43
30	18	21	20	19	18	20	22	18	17	28
31	37	32	33	34	35	35	35	30	30	50
32	45	28	46	43	34	49	37	33	49	62
33	27	26	23	25	21	25	30	22	24	37
34	35	22	39	35	31	40	37	25	39	51
35	38	32	41	39	30	43	42	32	39	55

Thesis #	SW Max	ATH Max	YGH Max	ALL Max	0/1s Max	2/3s Max	4/5s Max	15+ Max	14– Max	ALL G+VG
36	37	20	23	28	20	30	30	16	27	41
37	39	16	27	30	23	32	29	20	31	44
38	33	28	31	31	26	33	33	23	33	50
39	47	44	38	42	36	43	42	34	45	61
40	36	30	32	33	32	36	32	26	35	49
41	45	27	38	39	41	40	38	30	42	53
42	33	20	31	30	26	32	30	22	32	46
43	38	28	33	34	31	36	34	27	38	51
44	45	42	41	43	34	48	46	36	43	66
45	31	20	29	28	26	30	32	23	31	42
46	55	44	51	51	43	56	51	42	52	68
47	70	61	63	65	62	67	66	57	66	81
48	57	42	51	52	48	56	50	48	50	73

Thesis #	SW	ATH	YGH	ALL	0/1s	2/3s	4/5s	15+	14–	ALL
	Max	Max	Max	Max	Max	Max	Max	Max	Max	G+VG
49	55	43	46	49	44	54	48	43	51	70
50	40	33	34	36	29	45	39	27	35	55
51	27	17	21	23	21	28	20	17	25	37
52	33	20	32	31	25	46	28	23	32	45
53	45	33	43	42	32	56	42	34	45	63
54	42	34	38	39	39	51	39	33	38	61
55	28	19	26	26	20	39	29	20	29	41
56	41	33	33	36	27	50	38	32	40	53
57	58	39	52	52	46	62	47	41	57	77
58	32	36	31	32	31	35	37	28	34	48
59	29	15	24	24	20	36	21	17	31	33
60	54	52	52	53	45	63	51	46	53	76
61	27	23	28	27	23	38	26	21	29	42

Thesis #	SW Max	ATH Max	YGH Max	ALL Max	0/1s Max	2/3s Max	4/5s Max	15+ Max	14– Max	ALL G+VG
62	37	27	34	34	25	47	34	26	39	55
63	28	25	31	29	24	40	32	23	32	43
64	41	35	40	40	45	36	42	41	42	54
65	57	52	48	52	49	53	51	43	49	73
66	39	28	34	35	29	43	36	24	36	54
67	48	54	48	49	41	61	50	39	43	72
68	49	43	44	46	34	63	52	34	47	66
69	25	14	28	25	26	27	22	19	24	35
70	48	41	37	41	37	46	37	36	38	61
71	33	16	27	27	25	33	26	17	29	43
72	29	22	26	26	21	31	25	20	24	43
73	51	39	41	44	42	53	42	35	38	61
74	35	20	26	28	26	32	27	19	29	45

Thesis #	SW Max	ATH Max	YGH Max	ALL Max	0/1s Max	2/3s Max	4/5s Max	15+ Max	14– Max	ALL G+VG
75	36	34	33	34	32	44	31	26	32	50
76	33	24	24	27	25	33	28	20	24	41
77	53	29	44	45	47	40	44	35	37	62
78	38	32	37	37	36	34	38	28	31	52
79	35	22	29	30	25	41	33	21	29	48
80	41	33	32	35	29	45	35	29	33	53
81	34	23	30	30	24	43	29	23	27	47
82	34	36	19	27	26	29	29	24	22	43
83	43	32	35	37	30	48	33	27	32	58
84	32	23	30	30	25	41	32	21	29	49
85	36	26	31	32	26	47	27	25	29	51
86	47	30	42	42	36	50	43	28	39	61
87	36	25	28	30	28	34	32	22	26	47

Thesis #	SW Max	ATH Max	YGH Max	ALL Max	0/1s Max	2/3s Max	4/5s Max	15+ Max	14− Max	ALL G+VG
88	54	30	33	40	32	55	42	28	33	59
89	42	32	33	36	30	43	37	26	32	55
90	37	28	27	31	28	39	30	22	27	47
91	59	39	53	53	49	59	49	41	47	71
92	56	45	40	46	39	53	43	35	37	68
93	39	27	33	34	34	38	34	28	29	52
94	39	29	33	35	30	43	32	25	33	55
95	42	28	43	40	33	53	42	30	35	57
Average	42	33	37	38	34	43	39	31	38	55
Sample	158	66	222	446	159	222	65	263	175	446

Where: SW = Swords; ATH = Athenry; YGH = Youghal; ALL = Total

Max = % of maximum possible; G+VG = % good or very good; VG = % Very Good;

0/1s = 0 or 1 commitment out of 5, etc.

APPENDIX B — YOUTH GROUPS AND COMMUNITY GROUPS RELEVANT TO THIS TEXT

Project 2030 — Twentysomethings and Thirty-somethings

It's simply a way for people in or around their thirties with some links to the Church to get together and support one another by various activities; part of a larger network of similar groups.

There are regular programmes of events organised: social gatherings, walks, barbecues, pub lunches, Masses, céilí, days of retreat, daytrips and many other events. Events organised from ideas and initiatives from members.

The groups are sponsored by the Dehonians — the Sacred Heart Community who run the parish of Artane in Dublin, and are the brainchild of Fr Hugh Hanley, who initially set up and continues to support all the groups.

The Dehonians also look after centres and parishes in or around Glasgow, Liverpool, Manchester, and London. Project 2030 groups have been set up in all of these areas. The idea is to help us make contact with others of similar age and interests, and do things together.

Youth 2000

Youth 2000 is an international initiative of young people called to spread the good news of the Catholic faith. They pray together, they organise retreats and other spiritual events to help others to know and love God. The young people at the heart of this initiative offer what they have received to others of their generation.

Contact: Youth 2000, P.O. Box 8735, Tallaght, Dublin 24; e-mail: info@youth2000.ie; web: www.youth2000.ie.

Face Up

FaceUp.ie is the online presence of the monthly magazine *Face Up*, which is published by Redemptorist Publications. *Face Up* began publishing in January 2001 and is aimed at the 14–18-year-old age group and has the sub-title "For Teens Who Want Something Deeper".

At www.redemptoristpublications.com you will find the online edition of *Reality* and an archive of some previous material published in *Reality*.

Contact: *Face Up*, Redemptorist Publications, 75 Orwell Road, Rathgar, Dubin 6; Tel: 01-4922488 or 01-4067100; e-mail: info@faceup.ie.

Cell Groups

Fr Michael Hurley was among those who pioneered the launch of cell groups in Ireland. He has written widely about how they can most fruitfully benefit individuals and parishes. *Transforming Your Parish* (Columba Press, Dublin, 1998) provides very useful and inspirational help in the formation of cell groups. The secretary of the National Co-ordinating Body is Margaret Webb, 74 Larne Road, Carrickfergus, County Antrim, BT38 7EF; Tel: 04893-367861; e-mail: mags.webb@virgin.net.

Teen Spirit

Teen Spirit was set up in 2003 by Tipperary teenager Aaron Mullaney. Its wish is to "conquer" the following to the best of its ability:

Community Work/Christian Development

- The environment
- The elderly
- The disabled/special needs
- Prevention of cruelty to animals

Teen Spirit will also tackle such issues as homelessness, suicide, depression, drink and drugs. Money will be raised for charities.

Faith Development

- Bible studies
- Retreats and meetings with fellow Christians
- Life and Christian-related discussions
- Music, drama and the arts
- Recreation

Contact: aaron@thurlestown.com

Communio Edmund Rice

Based on creating small groups of people between 25 and 40 years of age, Communio is the initiative of the

Presentation Community. It encourages groups of 3–12 people to live out the vision and example of Edmund Rice in their daily lives.

Contact: Martin Kenneally, Presentation Brothers, Glasthule, County Dublin; Tel: 01-2801711.

The Dal Riada Centre

The Dal Riada Centre runs courses for young people on spiritual direction and contemporary issues. Course Director is Fr Martin O'Connor, LC and their approach has a healthy socialising element. Recent course titles include "Knowing Me Knowing You: what makes each of us tick", "Do Opposites Attract?" and "A Call to Guide: A mini-course on Spiritual Direction".

Contact: Dal Riada Centre, Avoca Avenue, Blackrock, Dublin; Tel 01-2889317; e-mail: hshekelton@arcol.org or dalriadacentre@arcol.org.

Peace Corps/Localise Groups

For more detailed information and start-up help re Peace Corps/Localise groups see www.pclocalise.com or contact the Development Officer, 52 Lr Rathmines Road, Dublin 6; Tel: 01-4964399; hotline: 087-6997281; e-mail info@pclocalise.com.

Youth and Family Encounter

This annual event features activities for young people of all ages, as well as crèche facilities. Tel: 01-2889317; e-mail: yfe.dublin@arcol.org

APPENDIX C — PAPAL TEXT MESSAGES

Since January 2003, mobile phone users in Italy have been just a text away from reading a brief daily inspirational message by Pope John Paul II. This service is now available in the English language in Ireland, the first country outside of Italy to receive the service.

The service in Ireland can be subscribed to by sending POPE ON as a text message to 53141. This will result in the Pope's "thought for the day" (taken from his homilies, messages and other writings) being delivered at 12.00 noon each day to the subscriber.

The short message service (SMS) will cost Irish users about €0.20 a day (including VAT), and is offered through all Irish mobile phone operators.

Bibliography

Bergin, Eilis PBVM and Fitzgerald, Eddie SDB (1997), *The Enneagram: The Quest for Self-Transcendence*, Dublin: SDB Media.

Box, Su (2003), *My Book of Prayers*, Lion.

Hahn, Scott (2003), *The Healing Power of Confession*, Darton, Longman and Todd.

Hurley, Michael (1998), *Transforming Your Parish*, Dublin: Columba Press.

Laurentin, Rene (1990), *The Apparitions of the Blessed Virgin Mary Today*, Dublin: Veritas.

Leon-Dufour, S.J., Xavier (1976), *The Gospels and the Jesus of History*, London: Collins.

Palmer, Helen (1988), *The Enneagram*, New York: Harper-Collins.

Wilson, A.N. (1998), *Pocket Canon Gospel of Matthew*, London: Canongate.

Wilson, Ian (1985), *Jesus: The Evidence*, London and Basingstoke: Pan.